Mastering Social Media Marketing: A Guide to Brand Growth and Engagement

By Anthony Colasante

Table of Contents

Introduction

- About This Book
- Why Social Media Marketing Matters
- Understanding the Power of Personal Branding

Chapter 1: The Foundations of Social Media Marketing

- The Evolution of Social Media
- Defining Your Brand Identity
- Setting Clear Goals and Objectives

Chapter 2: Choosing the Right Platforms

- Overview of Major Social Media Platforms
  - Facebook
  - Instagram
  - Twitter (X)
  - LinkedIn
  - TikTok
  - Pinterest
-

- Matching Your Brand with the Right Platforms
- Creating Platform-Specific Strategies

Chapter 3: Crafting a Winning Social Media Strategy

- Understanding Your Audience
- Content Creation and Curation
- The Art of Storytelling in Social Media
- Developing a Content Calendar

Chapter 4: Growing Your Audience

- Organic Growth Strategies
- Leveraging Hashtags and Trends
- Engaging with Your Followers
- Influencer Collaborations and Partnerships
- Running Contests and Giveaways

Chapter 5: Paid Social Media Advertising

- Understanding Paid Advertising on Social Media
- Budgeting and Ad Spend Strategies
- Crafting Compelling Ad Copy and Visuals

Analyzing Ad Performance and ROI

Chapter 6: Analytics and Measuring Success

- Key Metrics to Track on Each Platform
- Tools for Social Media Analytics
- Understanding Audience Insights
- Adjusting Strategies Based on Data

Chapter 7: Managing Your Online Reputation

- Handling Negative Feedback and Trolls
- Building and Maintaining Brand Trust
- Crisis Management on Social Media

Chapter 8: Advanced Strategies for Social Media Mastery

- The Power of Video Content
- Leveraging User-Generated Content
- Harnessing the Potential of Social Media Automation
- Exploring New and Emerging Platforms

Chapter 9: Integrating Social Media with Other Marketing Channels

-

- The Role of Social Media in Omnichannel Marketing
- Cross-Promotion Strategies
- Email Marketing and Social Media
- Integrating Social Media with SEO

Chapter 10: The Future of Social Media Marketing

- Trends to Watch in Social Media
- The Impact of AI and Machine Learning on Social Media
- Preparing Your Brand for the Future

Conclusion

- Recap of Key Strategies
- Next Steps for Your Social Media Journey
- Final Thoughts on Building a Successful Brand Online

Appendices

- Glossary of Social Media Terms
- Recommended Tools and Resources
- Social Media Content Templates
- Case Studies and Success Stories

References

-

Books, Articles, and Research Papers

Introduction

About This Book

Welcome to "Social Media Marketing Mastery: Building Your Brand and Audience." Whether you're a seasoned marketer, an entrepreneur, or just starting your journey into the world of social media, this book is designed to be your ultimate guide. The digital landscape has transformed how businesses and individuals interact with their audiences, and social media has become an essential tool for anyone looking to build a strong brand presence.

In today's interconnected world, the power of social media cannot be overstated. It's not just about posting pictures or sharing updates; it's about creating a narrative that resonates with your target audience, building meaningful relationships, and driving growth for your brand or business. This book will walk you through the key strategies and tools you need to succeed in this dynamic environment.

Why Social Media Marketing Matters

Social media is more than a trend; it's a fundamental shift in the way we communicate. With billions of people using platforms like Facebook, Instagram, LinkedIn, Twitter (X), and TikTok, the potential to reach and influence your audience is unparalleled. For businesses, social media offers a direct line to customers, providing insights into their needs, preferences, and behaviors. For individuals, it's an opportunity to build a personal brand, showcase expertise, and connect with like-minded people across the globe.

But with great opportunity comes great competition. To stand out in the crowded digital space, you need more than just a presence on social media—you need a strategy. This book will help you craft a personalized approach to social media marketing that aligns with your goals and leverages the unique strengths of each platform.

Understanding the Power of Personal Branding

Personal branding is no longer optional. Whether you're a business owner, a freelancer, or a professional, how you present yourself online can have a significant impact on your success. Your personal brand is your reputation—it's what people say about you when you're not in the room. In the digital age, this room is often a social media platform, where your audience is forming opinions about you based on the content you share and the way you interact.

This book will explore the concept of personal branding in depth, guiding you through the process of defining your brand identity, building your brand voice, and using social media to communicate your message effectively. Whether you're looking to boost your career, grow your business, or simply share your passions with the world, mastering personal branding on social media is crucial.

How to Use This Book

Each chapter of this book is designed to build upon the previous one, taking you from the basics of social media marketing to advanced strategies that will help you dominate your chosen platforms. You'll find practical advice, real-world examples, and actionable steps that you can implement immediately to start seeing results.

If you're new to social media marketing, I recommend starting from the beginning and working your way through the chapters in order. For those with more experience, feel free to jump to the sections that are most relevant to your current needs.

Social media is a constantly evolving field, and this book aims to equip you with the foundational knowledge and adaptable strategies necessary to thrive in it. By the end of this journey, you'll have a solid understanding of how to use social media to build your brand, grow your audience, and achieve your business goals.

Let's get started on your path to social media marketing mastery!

Chapter 1: The Foundations of Social Media Marketing

The Evolution of Social Media

Social media has come a long way since its inception. What began as simple platforms for people to connect with friends and share personal updates has transformed into a powerful tool for communication, marketing, and brand building. Understanding the evolution of social media is essential to appreciating its current impact and potential for your brand.

The Early Days

The roots of social media can be traced back to the late 1990s with the emergence of platforms like Six Degrees and LiveJournal, which allowed users to create profiles and connect with others online. However, it wasn't until the early 2000s that social media began to take shape in the way we know it today. Platforms like MySpace and Friendster introduced the concept of social networking on a larger scale, allowing users to create more detailed profiles, share content, and build communities.

The Rise of Major Platforms

The mid-2000s marked a significant turning point with the launch of Facebook, Twitter, and LinkedIn. These platforms revolutionized how people interacted online, shifting from simply connecting with friends to building networks, sharing ideas, and engaging with content. Facebook, in particular, became the first platform to reach a billion users, setting the stage for social media to become a dominant force in the digital age.

Twitter introduced the concept of microblogging, where users could share short updates (tweets) with their followers, fostering real-time communication and information sharing. LinkedIn carved out a niche as the go-to platform for professionals, allowing users to network, job hunt, and showcase their expertise.

The Visual Era and Beyond

The 2010s brought about the rise of visual-based platforms like Instagram, Snapchat, and Pinterest. These platforms emphasized images and videos over text, appealing to users' desire for quick, visually engaging content. Instagram's success in particular highlighted the importance of aesthetics and storytelling in social media marketing.

As technology continued to advance, video content gained prominence, leading to the rise of platforms like YouTube and TikTok. Video became a preferred medium for brands and individuals to connect with audiences, providing a more immersive and engaging experience.

The Current Landscape

Today, social media is an integral part of daily life for billions of people worldwide. It has expanded beyond personal communication to include everything from e-commerce and customer service to entertainment and news. Social media platforms are now sophisticated ecosystems that offer brands unparalleled opportunities to reach, engage, and convert audiences.

However, with these opportunities come challenges. The landscape is constantly evolving, with new platforms emerging and algorithms changing frequently. To succeed in social media marketing, it's crucial to stay informed about these trends and be adaptable in your strategies.

Defining Your Brand Identity

Before you dive into creating content and engaging with your audience on social media, it's essential to define your brand identity. Your brand identity is the foundation upon which all your marketing efforts will be built. It encompasses your values, mission, and the overall image you want to project to the world.

What is Brand Identity?

Brand identity is the unique combination of visual elements, messaging, and personality traits that distinguish your brand from others. It's how your audience perceives you and what they think of when they hear your brand's name. A strong brand identity helps you establish a connection with your audience, build trust, and create a memorable impression.

Key Elements of Brand Identity

1. **Brand Values:** What does your brand stand for? Your values are the core principles that guide your business decisions and actions. They reflect what's important to you and your audience.
2. **Mission Statement:** Your mission statement is a concise declaration of your brand's purpose. It should communicate what you aim to achieve and how you intend to make a difference in the lives of your audience.
3. **Brand Personality:** Just like people, brands have personalities. Is your brand fun and playful, or serious and professional? Defining your brand's personality helps you create a consistent tone and style across all your marketing efforts.
4. **Visual Identity:** This includes your logo, color scheme, typography, and any other visual elements that represent your brand. Your visual identity should be cohesive and easily recognizable.
5. **Unique Selling Proposition (USP):** Your USP is what sets you apart from your competitors. It's the unique benefit or value that only your brand can offer to your audience.

Creating a Brand Identity for Social Media

When defining your brand identity for social media, consider how each platform's unique features can be leveraged to enhance your brand's image. For example, Instagram's focus on visuals makes it ideal for showcasing your brand's aesthetic, while Twitter's emphasis on brevity allows you to convey your brand's voice in short, impactful messages.

It's also important to maintain consistency across all platforms. While you may tailor your content to fit the platform, your brand's core identity should remain the same. This consistency helps reinforce your brand's image and makes it easier for your audience to recognize and remember you.

Setting Clear Goals and Objectives

Once you've defined your brand identity, the next step is to set clear goals and objectives for your social media marketing efforts. Without a clear direction, it's easy to get lost in the noise and fail to achieve meaningful results.

Why Goals and Objectives Matter

Setting goals and objectives provides you with a roadmap for your social media strategy. They give you a sense of direction, help you measure success, and ensure that your efforts are aligned with your overall business goals. Without clear goals, it's difficult to determine whether your social media marketing is effective or if you need to adjust your approach.

Types of Social Media Goals

There are several types of goals you can set for your social media marketing, depending on your brand's needs and priorities. Here are some common goals to consider:

1. **Brand Awareness:** Increase the visibility of your brand and reach a larger audience.

2. **Engagement:** Encourage interactions with your content, such as likes, comments, shares, and direct messages.
3. **Lead Generation:** Attract potential customers and gather their contact information for future marketing efforts.
4. **Conversions:** Drive sales, sign-ups, or other desired actions that contribute to your bottom line.
5. **Customer Service:** Use social media as a platform to provide support and address customer inquiries.
6. **Community Building:** Foster a sense of community among your audience by encouraging discussions and interactions.

Setting SMART Objectives

To make your goals actionable, it's helpful to use the SMART framework when setting objectives. SMART stands for Specific, Measurable, Achievable, Relevant, and Time-bound. Here's how you can apply this framework to your social media objectives:

- **Specific:** Clearly define what you want to achieve. For example, instead of saying "increase engagement," specify that you want to "increase the average number of comments on Instagram posts by 20%."
- **Measurable:** Ensure that you can track and measure your progress. Use metrics such as follower count, engagement rate, or conversion rate to quantify your objectives.
- **Achievable:** Set realistic objectives that are within your reach. Consider your current resources, audience size, and industry benchmarks when setting goals.
- **Relevant:** Align your objectives with your overall business goals. Each objective should contribute to your broader marketing strategy and brand vision.

- **Time-bound:** Set a deadline for achieving your objectives. This helps create a sense of urgency and keeps you focused on your goals.

Tracking and Adjusting Your Goals

Setting goals is only the beginning. It's equally important to track your progress and adjust your strategy as needed. Use analytics tools to monitor key performance indicators (KPIs) related to your goals and assess whether you're on track to achieve them. If you're not seeing the desired results, be prepared to tweak your approach and experiment with different tactics.

In this chapter, you've learned about the evolution of social media, the importance of defining your brand identity, and the process of setting clear goals and objectives. With a strong foundation in place, you're now ready to move forward with creating a social media strategy that will help you build your brand and grow your audience.

Chapter 2: Choosing the Right Platforms

Choosing the right social media platforms for your brand is a crucial step in your social media marketing strategy. Each platform offers unique features and attracts different types of audiences, so it's essential to understand their strengths and weaknesses. In this chapter, we'll explore the major social media platforms and help you decide which ones are the best fit for your brand. We'll also discuss how to create platform-specific strategies to maximize your impact.

Overview of Major Social Media Platforms

Facebook

Audience: With over 2.8 billion monthly active users, Facebook is the largest social media platform in the world. It attracts a diverse audience, but the majority of users are between the ages of 25 and 34. Facebook is ideal for brands targeting a broad demographic and those who want to build a community around their products or services.

Key Features:

- **Facebook Pages:** Create a dedicated page for your brand where you can post updates, share content, and interact with your audience.
- **Groups:** Build and engage with communities of like-minded individuals around shared interests or topics.
- **Facebook Ads:** Leverage Facebook's powerful advertising platform to reach specific audiences with targeted ads.
-

Live Video: Connect with your audience in real-time through live streaming.

Best For: Building brand awareness, engaging with a broad audience, running targeted ad campaigns, and fostering communities.

Instagram

Audience: Instagram has over 1 billion monthly active users, with a strong focus on younger demographics, particularly those aged 18-34. The platform is highly visual, making it ideal for brands with strong visual content, such as fashion, beauty, travel, and lifestyle brands.

Key Features:

- **Stories:** Share ephemeral content that disappears after 24 hours, perfect for behind-the-scenes glimpses or time-sensitive promotions.
- **IGTV and Reels:** Post longer-form videos or short, engaging clips to capture your audience's attention.
- **Shopping:** Tag products in your posts and stories to enable direct purchases within the app.
- **Hashtags:** Increase your content's discoverability by using relevant hashtags.

Best For: Brands that can showcase their products or services visually, engage with younger audiences, and leverage influencer partnerships.

Twitter (X)

Audience: Twitter has around 330 million monthly active users, with a strong presence among professionals, journalists, and influencers. The platform is known for its real-time nature, making it ideal for brands that want to engage in conversations, share news, and connect with audiences quickly.

Key Features:

- **Tweets:** Share short updates, links, and media in 280 characters or less.
- **Threads:** Create a series of connected tweets to tell a more extended story or provide more information.
- **Trending Topics:** Join conversations around trending hashtags and topics to increase visibility.
- **Twitter Ads:** Promote tweets, accounts, or trends to a targeted audience.

Best For: Brands that want to engage in real-time conversations, share news, and connect with influencers or industry professionals.

LinkedIn

Audience: LinkedIn has over 740 million members, primarily consisting of professionals and businesses. It's the go-to platform for B2B marketing, networking, and thought leadership. LinkedIn is ideal for brands that target other businesses, professionals, or anyone looking to establish themselves as an industry leader.

Key Features:

- **Company Pages:** Showcase your business, post updates, and engage with your professional network.
- **LinkedIn Groups:** Participate in or create groups around specific industries or topics to connect with like-minded professionals.
- **LinkedIn Ads:** Run targeted ad campaigns to reach professionals based on job title, industry, company size, and more.
- **Publishing Platform:** Share long-form articles and insights to establish thought leadership.

Best For: B2B brands, professional services, recruitment, and industry thought leadership.

TikTok

Audience: TikTok has quickly become one of the most popular social media platforms, especially among Gen Z and millennials. With over 1 billion monthly active users, TikTok is a video-first platform where creativity and authenticity are key. It's ideal for brands that want to reach a younger audience and create viral content.

Key Features:

- **Short-Form Videos:** Create engaging videos up to 3 minutes long with music, filters, and effects.
- **Challenges:** Participate in or create challenges to encourage user-generated content and increase visibility.

- **TikTok Ads:** Run targeted ad campaigns that blend seamlessly into the platform's content.

- **Live Streaming:** Engage with your audience in real-time through live videos.

Best For: Brands targeting younger demographics, creating viral content, and leveraging trends for maximum engagement.

Pinterest

Audience: Pinterest has over 450 million monthly active users, with a strong presence among women, particularly those aged 25-54. Pinterest is a highly visual platform that functions as a search engine for inspiration, making it ideal for brands in the fashion, home decor, food, and DIY spaces.

Key Features:

- **Pins:** Share images and videos that link back to your website or other content.

- **Boards:** Organize your pins into themed collections, making it easier for users to find and save your content.

- **Pinterest Ads:** Promote pins to reach a broader audience and drive traffic to your website.

- **Rich Pins:** Enhance your pins with additional information, such as product details or recipe ingredients.

Best For: Brands that can create visually appealing content, drive traffic to their websites, and inspire users through DIY, fashion, home decor, and lifestyle content.

Matching Your Brand with the Right Platforms

Choosing the right social media platforms for your brand is crucial to maximizing your marketing efforts. Not every platform will be suitable for your brand, so it's important to consider your target audience, the type of content you create, and your overall marketing goals.

Understand Your Audience

Start by understanding where your target audience spends their time online. Research the demographics of each platform to identify where your potential customers are most active. For example, if your target audience is predominantly young adults, TikTok and Instagram may be more effective platforms for your brand than LinkedIn.

Consider Your Content Type

The type of content you create will also influence your platform choice. If your brand relies heavily on visual content, such as fashion or food, Instagram and Pinterest are natural choices. If you focus on thought leadership and B2B marketing, LinkedIn might be more appropriate.

Align with Your Goals

Your social media goals should align with the platforms you choose. If your primary goal is to build brand awareness, Facebook's broad reach might be beneficial. If you're looking to generate leads or drive traffic to your website, Pinterest and LinkedIn's advertising capabilities could be more effective.

Assess Your Resources

Managing multiple social media platforms can be time-consuming. Consider your team's capacity and resources when choosing platforms. It's better to be highly active and engaged on a few platforms than to spread yourself too thin across many.

Creating Platform-Specific Strategies

Once you've chosen the right platforms for your brand, the next step is to develop platform-specific strategies. Each platform has its own unique features, audience behavior, and content formats, so it's important to tailor your approach accordingly.

Facebook Strategy

- **Content Mix:** Use a mix of text, images, videos, and links to keep your content varied and engaging.
- **Community Building:** Create and nurture Facebook Groups around topics relevant to your brand.
- **Paid Advertising:** Use Facebook's targeting options to run highly specific ad campaigns that reach your ideal audience.
- **Engagement:** Respond to comments and messages promptly to build a strong relationship with your audience.

Instagram Strategy

- **Visual Consistency:** Maintain a consistent aesthetic by using the same filters, color schemes, and themes across your posts.
- **Stories:** Use Instagram Stories for more casual, behind-the-scenes content that disappears after 24 hours.
-

- **Influencer Partnerships:** Collaborate with influencers to reach a broader audience and enhance your brand's credibility.
- **Hashtag Strategy:** Use a mix of popular and niche hashtags to increase the discoverability of your content.

Twitter (X) Strategy

- **Timely Updates:** Share real-time updates, news, and industry insights to keep your audience informed.
- **Engage in Conversations:** Join trending topics and participate in relevant conversations to increase visibility.
- **Use of Threads:** Create tweet threads to tell a longer story or provide in-depth information on a topic.
- **Monitor Mentions:** Keep track of brand mentions and respond to users to foster engagement and build relationships.

LinkedIn Strategy

- **Thought Leadership:** Share long-form articles and insights to establish yourself as an expert in your field.
- **Professional Networking:** Connect with industry leaders, potential clients, and partners to expand your professional network.
- **Targeted Ads:** Use LinkedIn's advertising options to reach decision-makers and professionals in your target industry.

Employee Advocacy: Encourage employees to share company content and engage with your brand on LinkedIn to increase reach.

TikTok Strategy

- **Trendy Content:** Stay up-to-date with the latest TikTok trends and create content that aligns with them to increase visibility.
- **Challenges:** Participate in or create TikTok challenges to encourage user-generated content and boost engagement.
- **Authenticity:** Focus on creating authentic, relatable content that resonates with TikTok's younger audience.
- **Influencer Collaborations:** Partner with TikTok influencers to reach a larger audience and build credibility.

Pinterest Strategy

- **Content Organization:** Organize your content into themed boards that make it easy for users to find and save your pins.
- **Rich Pins:** Use Rich Pins to provide additional context and information about your products or services.
- **Search Optimization:** Optimize your pins and boards with relevant keywords to improve search visibility on Pinterest.
- **Seasonal Content:** Create and promote seasonal content that aligns with your audience's interests and behaviors.

In this chapter, you've learned about the major social media platforms, how to choose the right ones for your brand, and how to create platform-specific strategies. By selecting the platforms that align with your audience, content, and goals, and tailoring your approach to each platform's unique features, you'll be well on your way to social media marketing success.

Chapter 3: Crafting a Winning Social Media Strategy

Creating a successful social media strategy is about more than just posting content. It's about understanding your audience, telling compelling stories, and consistently delivering value through a well-planned approach. In this chapter, we'll explore the key elements of crafting a winning social media strategy, including understanding your audience, content creation and curation, the art of storytelling, and developing a content calendar.

Understanding Your Audience

To create content that resonates, you first need to understand who your audience is and what they care about. Knowing your audience's demographics, preferences, and behavior will help you tailor your content to meet their needs and expectations.

Demographics and Psychographics

Start by gathering demographic information about your audience, such as age, gender, location, education, and income level. This data will help you identify the general characteristics of your audience and tailor your content to suit their needs.

Beyond demographics, delve into psychographics, which includes your audience's interests, values, lifestyles, and pain points. Psychographics provide deeper insights into why your audience behaves the way they do, allowing you to create more targeted and emotionally resonant content.

Audience Personas

Create detailed audience personas that represent your ideal customers. A persona is a fictional character that embodies the characteristics of your target audience. Each persona should include:

- **Name and Background:** A fictional name and brief background to humanize the persona.
- **Demographics:** Age, gender, location, occupation, education level, etc.
- **Goals and Challenges:** What are their primary goals? What challenges do they face?
- **Interests and Values:** What are they passionate about? What do they value most?
- **Preferred Content:** What type of content do they consume? Which platforms do they use?

By creating personas, you can better visualize who you're speaking to and tailor your content accordingly.

Behavioral Insights

Use analytics tools to track your audience's behavior on social media. Pay attention to metrics such as engagement rates, click-through rates, and the time of day your audience is most active. This data will help you refine your strategy by understanding what type of content performs best and when to post it.

Listening to Your Audience

Social listening is the practice of monitoring social media channels for mentions of your brand, competitors, or related topics. It allows you to gain insights into what your audience is saying about your industry, products, and services. Use social listening tools to track conversations and identify trends that can inform your content strategy.

Content Creation and Curation

Once you have a clear understanding of your audience, the next step is to create and curate content that engages, educates, and entertains. Your content should reflect your brand identity and resonate with your audience, while also serving your overall marketing goals.

Content Creation

Content creation is the process of generating original content that aligns with your brand's voice and goals. Here are some key types of content to consider:

- **Educational Content:** Create content that educates your audience about topics related to your industry. This could include how-to guides, tutorials, or informative articles.
- **Entertaining Content:** Engage your audience with fun, light-hearted content such as memes, quizzes, or behind-the-scenes videos.
- **Inspirational Content:** Share stories, quotes, or testimonials that inspire and motivate your audience.
- **Promotional Content:** Highlight your products, services, or special offers. Ensure that promotional content is balanced with other types of content to avoid appearing overly sales-focused.
- **User-Generated Content:** Encourage your audience to create and share content related to your brand. User-generated content is highly authentic and can boost trust and engagement.

Content Curation

Content curation involves selecting and sharing valuable content created by others. Curated content should complement your original content and provide additional value to your audience. Here's how to curate content effectively:

- **Select Quality Content:** Choose high-quality content from credible sources that align with your brand's values and interests.
- **Add Your Perspective:** When sharing curated content, include your own commentary or insights to add value and provide context for your audience.
- **Diversify Your Sources:** Curate content from a variety of sources, including industry blogs, news sites, and influencers, to provide a well-rounded perspective.
- **Maintain a Balance:** Balance curated content with original content to ensure your brand's voice remains prominent.

Visual and Multimedia Content

In today's social media landscape, visual content is more important than ever. Incorporate images, videos, infographics, and other multimedia elements into your content strategy to capture attention and drive engagement. Visual content is especially effective on platforms like Instagram, Pinterest, and TikTok, where aesthetics and creativity are key.

The Art of Storytelling in Social Media

Storytelling is a powerful tool for building connections with your audience. By telling compelling stories, you can evoke emotions, create memorable experiences, and convey your brand's message in a way that resonates deeply with your audience.

Why Storytelling Matters

Stories are memorable and relatable. They allow you to convey complex ideas in a way that's easy to understand and emotionally engaging. Through storytelling, you can humanize your brand, making it more relatable and trustworthy.

Elements of a Great Story

To craft a compelling story, consider the following elements:

- **Character:** Every story needs a protagonist, whether it's your brand, a customer, or an employee. The character should be relatable and face challenges that your audience can empathize with.
- **Conflict:** Conflict is what makes a story interesting. It could be a problem your brand solves, a challenge your customer overcomes, or a journey your company has undertaken.
- **Resolution:** The resolution is where the conflict is resolved, and the story comes to a satisfying conclusion. This could be the success of your product, the achievement of a goal, or the fulfillment of a promise.
- **Emotion:** Emotion is what connects your audience to the story. Whether it's joy, inspiration, or empathy, evoking emotions helps your audience connect with your brand on a deeper level.

Incorporating Storytelling into Your Content

- **Customer Stories:** Share testimonials, case studies, or success stories from your customers. Highlight how your product or service has made a difference in their lives.
- **Brand Journey:** Tell the story of your brand's founding, growth, and evolution. Share the challenges you've faced and the milestones you've achieved.
- **Behind-the-Scenes:** Give your audience a glimpse into the behind-the-scenes activities of your business. This could include your team's daily routines, product development, or company culture.
- **User-Generated Stories:** Encourage your audience to share their own stories related to your brand. Feature their stories on your social media channels to build community and trust.

Developing a Content Calendar

A content calendar is a planning tool that helps you organize and schedule your social media content in advance. It ensures that your content is consistent, timely, and aligned with your overall strategy.

Why You Need a Content Calendar

A content calendar provides structure and helps you maintain a consistent posting schedule. It allows you to plan content around key dates, events, and campaigns, ensuring that your social media activities are well-coordinated. Additionally, a content calendar helps you manage resources more effectively by allowing you to plan ahead and avoid last-minute content creation.

Steps to Create a Content Calendar

1. **Set Goals:** Start by defining the goals you want to achieve with your content. These goals should align with your overall social media strategy and business objectives.
2. **Identify Key Dates:** Identify important dates, such as holidays, product launches, and industry events, that you want to plan content around.
3. **Plan Content Themes:** Choose content themes for each week or month based on your goals, audience preferences, and key dates. Themes could include topics like education, inspiration, or promotion.
4. **Create a Posting Schedule:** Determine how often you want to post on each platform. Consider your audience's behavior and platform-specific best practices when setting your posting frequency.
5. **Assign Content Types:** Decide on the types of content you'll create for each platform, such as blog posts, videos, infographics, or user-generated content. Assign specific content types to each day or week.
6. **Allocate Resources:** Determine who will be responsible for creating, curating, and publishing content. Assign tasks to team members and ensure that deadlines are met.
7. **Monitor and Adjust:** Regularly review the performance of your content and adjust your calendar as needed. Use analytics to identify what's working and make data-driven decisions to optimize your strategy.

Tools for Managing Your Content Calendar

There are several tools available to help you create and manage your content calendar, including:

- **Google Calendar:** A simple and accessible option for planning and scheduling content.

- **Trello:** A visual project management tool that allows you to organize content ideas, assign tasks, and track progress.
- **Hootsuite:** A social media management platform that includes a content calendar feature, allowing you to schedule posts across multiple platforms.
- **Asana:** A project management tool that helps you plan, organize, and track your content creation process.

In this chapter, you've learned how to understand your audience, create and curate content, harness the power of storytelling, and develop a content calendar. These elements are the building blocks of a winning social media strategy that will help you engage your audience, build your brand, and achieve your marketing goals.

Chapter 4: Growing Your Audience

Growing your audience is a critical aspect of a successful social media strategy. A larger, engaged audience increases brand awareness, boosts credibility, and creates more opportunities for conversions. In this chapter, we'll explore effective strategies for organic growth, the power of hashtags and trends, the importance of engagement, leveraging influencer collaborations, and running contests and giveaways.

Organic Growth Strategies

Organic growth refers to the process of increasing your audience without paid advertising. While it can be slower than paid methods, organic growth builds a loyal and engaged audience that is genuinely interested in your brand. Here are some key strategies for achieving organic growth:

Consistency is Key

Posting consistently is one of the most important factors in growing your audience organically. Regular updates keep your audience engaged and signal to social media algorithms that your content is active and relevant. Develop a posting schedule based on your content calendar and stick to it.

Quality Over Quantity

While consistency is important, the quality of your content is paramount. High-quality content that provides value to your audience—whether through education, entertainment, or inspiration—is more likely to be shared, liked, and commented on. Focus on creating content that resonates with your audience and reflects your brand's values.

Optimize Your Profile

Your social media profiles are often the first impression potential followers have of your brand. Ensure that your profile is fully optimized with a clear, compelling bio, a professional profile picture, and links to your website or other key destinations. Use keywords relevant to your industry in your bio to make your profile more discoverable.

Engage with Your Community

Building a community around your brand is essential for organic growth. Respond to comments, answer questions, and engage in conversations with your followers. Show appreciation for their support by liking and sharing user-generated content. The more you engage with your audience, the more likely they are to become loyal followers.

Cross-Promotion

Leverage your presence on other platforms to promote your social media accounts. For example, if you have a strong email list, include links to your social media profiles in your newsletters. If you have a blog, embed social media posts or include share buttons. Cross-promotion helps drive traffic to your social media profiles from other channels where you already have an audience.

Leveraging Hashtags and Trends

Hashtags and trends are powerful tools for increasing your content's visibility and reaching a broader audience. By strategically using hashtags and participating in trending conversations, you can attract new followers who are interested in your content.

Hashtag Strategy

Hashtags categorize your content and make it discoverable to users searching for or following those tags. To effectively use hashtags:

- **Research Relevant Hashtags:** Identify popular and relevant hashtags in your industry. Use tools like Hashtagify or RiteTag to discover trending hashtags and analyze their performance.

- **Mix of Popular and Niche Hashtags:** Use a combination of widely popular hashtags and more specific, niche hashtags. Popular hashtags can increase your reach, while niche hashtags help you connect with a more targeted audience.

- **Branded Hashtags:** Create a unique hashtag for your brand that encourages user-generated content. For example, if your brand sells fitness apparel, you might create a hashtag like #FitWith[YourBrandName] to inspire followers to share photos of themselves wearing your products.

- **Limit the Number of Hashtags:** While it can be tempting to use as many hashtags as possible, too many can look spammy. Aim for 5-10 relevant hashtags per post, depending on the platform.

Participating in Trends

Trends are topics or challenges that gain widespread popularity on social media, often for a limited time. Participating in trends can significantly boost your content's visibility:

- **Stay Updated:** Keep an eye on trending topics and challenges on the platforms you use. Twitter's trending section, TikTok's Discover page, and Instagram's Explore tab are good places to start.

- **Be Authentic:** Only participate in trends that align with your brand values and audience interests. Forced participation can come across as inauthentic.

- **Add Your Unique Spin:** When joining a trend, try to add your brand's unique voice or perspective to stand out. Whether it's a clever twist on a popular meme or a brand-specific take on a challenge, originality is key.

Engaging with Your Followers

Engagement is the foundation of building a loyal and active social media following. The more you engage with your followers, the stronger the relationship you'll build, leading to higher retention rates and more word-of-mouth referrals.

Respond to Comments and Messages

Make it a priority to respond to comments and direct messages in a timely manner. Whether it's a question, a compliment, or constructive criticism, acknowledging your followers shows that you value their input. This can turn casual followers into loyal advocates for your brand.

Ask Questions and Encourage Dialogue

Encourage your audience to engage by asking open-ended questions in your posts. For example, if you're a food brand, you might post a picture of a dish and ask, "What's your favorite ingredient to cook with?" Questions invite your audience to share their opinions and experiences, fostering a sense of community.

Host Q&A Sessions

Q&A sessions, either through live video or in your stories, allow your audience to interact with you directly. These sessions provide value by answering your followers' burning questions and can be an effective way to boost engagement. Promote your Q&A sessions in advance to encourage participation.

Acknowledge Your Followers

Highlighting your followers can create a stronger connection. For instance, you can feature a "follower of the week" or share user-generated content that showcases your product. This not only builds goodwill but also encourages more followers to engage in the hopes of being featured.

Influencer Collaborations and Partnerships

Influencer marketing is a powerful way to reach new audiences and build credibility. By partnering with influencers who align with your brand, you can tap into their follower base and expand your reach organically.

Choosing the Right Influencers

Not all influencers are created equal. When selecting influencers to collaborate with, consider the following factors:

- **Relevance:** The influencer should align with your brand's values and appeal to your target audience. For example, if you're a skincare brand, partnering with beauty influencers makes sense.
- **Engagement Rate:** Look beyond the follower count and consider the influencer's engagement rate. An influencer with a smaller but highly engaged audience may be more valuable than one with a large but passive following.
-

Content Quality: Review the influencer's content to ensure it meets your brand's standards. The quality of their posts, captions, and overall aesthetic should align with your brand identity.

-

Authenticity: Choose influencers who have a genuine connection to your brand or industry. Authentic endorsements are more likely to resonate with their audience.

Types of Collaborations

There are various ways to collaborate with influencers, depending on your goals:

-

Sponsored Posts: Pay influencers to create content that features your product or service. Sponsored posts can take the form of photos, videos, or stories.

-

Product Reviews: Send your product to influencers in exchange for an honest review. This type of collaboration works well for building trust and credibility.

-

Giveaways: Partner with influencers to run contests and giveaways that encourage their followers to engage with your brand.

-

Takeovers: Allow influencers to "take over" your social media account for a day. This can give your audience a fresh perspective and introduce new content ideas.

Measuring Success

After the collaboration, analyze the results to measure success. Track metrics such as engagement, follower growth, website traffic, and conversions to determine the impact of the partnership. Use this data to refine your future influencer marketing strategies.

Running Contests and Giveaways

Contests and giveaways are highly effective at driving engagement, attracting new followers, and rewarding your existing audience. They create excitement around your brand and can lead to a significant increase in followers in a short period of time.

Planning a Successful Contest or Giveaway

To run a successful contest or giveaway, follow these steps:

- **Set Clear Goals:** Determine what you want to achieve, whether it's increasing brand awareness, growing your follower count, or promoting a new product.
- **Choose the Right Prize:** The prize should be valuable enough to encourage participation but relevant to your brand. For example, if you're a fitness brand, offering a free workout program or gym gear would be appropriate.
- **Define the Rules:** Clearly outline the rules for entering the contest. Common entry requirements include following your account, liking a post, tagging friends, or sharing content.
- **Promote the Contest:** Use all your social media platforms to promote the contest. Consider using paid ads to reach a broader audience.
-

Engage During the Contest: Keep the excitement going by engaging with participants during the contest. Respond to comments, share entries, and provide updates.

Announcing Winners and Following Up

Once the contest ends, announce the winners promptly and transparently. Publicly congratulating the winners can boost your brand's credibility and encourage future participation. Follow up by engaging with all participants, thanking them for entering, and encouraging them to stay connected for future contests and content.

Legal Considerations

Be aware of the legal requirements for running contests and giveaways. Different countries and platforms have specific rules regarding disclosures, eligibility, and prize distribution. Make sure to comply with all relevant regulations to avoid legal issues.

In this chapter, you've learned how to grow your audience through organic strategies, leverage hashtags and trends, engage with your followers, collaborate with influencers, and run effective contests and giveaways. By implementing these strategies, you'll be well on your way to building a larger, more engaged audience that is invested in your brand's success.

Chapter 5: Paid Social Media Advertising

Paid social media advertising is a powerful tool for reaching a broader audience, driving traffic, and generating conversions. Unlike organic strategies, paid advertising allows you to target specific demographics, interests, and behaviors, giving you greater control over who sees your content. In this chapter, we'll explore the fundamentals of paid social media advertising, how to budget and manage your ad spend, tips for crafting compelling ad copy and visuals, and how to analyze ad performance to maximize return on investment (ROI).

Understanding Paid Advertising on Social Media

Paid social media advertising involves promoting your content or brand through paid placements on social media platforms. These ads can appear in various formats, including sponsored posts, display ads, video ads, and more. The primary advantage of paid advertising is the ability to target specific audiences, ensuring that your content reaches the right people at the right time.

Types of Paid Social Media Ads

Different social media platforms offer various types of ads, each with unique features and benefits. Here are some common ad formats across major platforms:

- **Facebook Ads:** Includes image ads, video ads, carousel ads (multiple images or videos in a single ad), slideshow ads, and collection ads (a full-screen experience featuring products). Facebook also offers lead ads, which allow users to fill out forms directly within the ad.
-

- **Instagram Ads:** Similar to Facebook, Instagram offers photo ads, video ads, carousel ads, and collection ads. Additionally, Instagram Stories ads allow you to place full-screen ads in between user stories.
- **Twitter Ads:** Twitter offers promoted tweets, promoted accounts, and promoted trends. These ads can include images, videos, and polls, and are designed to increase visibility and engagement.
- **LinkedIn Ads:** LinkedIn's advertising options include sponsored content, sponsored InMail (personalized messages sent to LinkedIn users), text ads, and dynamic ads (personalized ads that adapt to individual users).
- **TikTok Ads:** TikTok offers in-feed ads (similar to Instagram Stories), branded hashtag challenges, branded effects (custom stickers or filters), and TopView ads (full-screen videos that appear when users open the app).

- **Pinterest Ads:** Pinterest's advertising options include promoted pins, promoted video pins, carousel ads, and shopping ads. These ads are integrated seamlessly into users' feeds, making them highly effective for driving traffic and sales.

Benefits of Paid Social Media Advertising

- **Targeted Reach:** Paid ads allow you to reach specific audiences based on demographics, interests, behaviors, and more.
- **Increased Visibility:** Paid ads can significantly increase your brand's visibility, especially in competitive industries.

Quick Results: Unlike organic strategies, paid ads can generate immediate results, such as website traffic, leads, and sales.

-

Scalability: Paid advertising is highly scalable, allowing you to increase or decrease your ad spend based on performance and budget.

Setting Objectives for Paid Ads

Before launching a paid ad campaign, it's crucial to define your objectives. Common objectives include:

-

Brand Awareness: Increase the visibility of your brand to a broader audience.

-

Traffic: Drive users to your website, landing page, or online store.

-

Engagement: Encourage likes, comments, shares, and other interactions with your content.

-

Lead Generation: Capture potential customers' information for future marketing efforts.

-

Conversions: Drive specific actions, such as purchases, sign-ups, or downloads.

Clearly defined objectives will guide your ad creation and help you measure the success of your campaigns.

Budgeting and Ad Spend Strategies

Effective budgeting and ad spend management are essential to maximizing the impact of your paid social media campaigns. A well-planned budget ensures that you allocate resources efficiently and achieve your marketing goals without overspending.

Setting Your Budget

When setting your budget, consider the following factors:

- **Overall Marketing Budget:** Determine how much of your overall marketing budget you can allocate to paid social media advertising. This will depend on your business size, industry, and marketing priorities.
- **Campaign Objectives:** Your budget should align with your campaign objectives. For example, a brand awareness campaign may require a larger budget to reach a broad audience, while a lead generation campaign may need a more focused budget.
- **Audience Size:** The size of your target audience can influence your budget. Reaching a larger audience generally requires a higher ad spend, especially on platforms with competitive bidding.
- **Duration of Campaign:** The length of your campaign will also impact your budget. A longer campaign will require a sustained budget, while a shorter, time-sensitive campaign may require a more concentrated spend.

Ad Spend Strategies

Different ad spend strategies can help you optimize your budget and achieve your objectives:

-

- **Daily Budget vs. Lifetime Budget:** Most platforms allow you to set either a daily budget (the maximum amount you'll spend each day) or a lifetime budget (the total amount you'll spend over the course of the campaign). A daily budget is useful for maintaining consistent ad exposure, while a lifetime budget allows for more flexibility in how your budget is spent over time.
- **Manual vs. Automated Bidding:** Platforms like Facebook and Google offer both manual and automated bidding options. Manual bidding gives you control over how much you're willing to pay for each click, impression, or conversion. Automated bidding uses algorithms to adjust your bids in real-time to achieve the best results within your budget. Experiment with both options to determine which works best for your goals.
- **A/B Testing:** A/B testing involves running multiple versions of an ad to see which performs better. By testing different ad creatives, headlines, and targeting options, you can identify the most effective combination and allocate more budget to the top-performing ads.
- **Retargeting:** Retargeting allows you to show ads to users who have already interacted with your brand, such as visiting your website or engaging with your content. Retargeting is often more cost-effective than targeting cold audiences, as these users are already familiar with your brand and more likely to convert.

Crafting Compelling Ad Copy and Visuals

The success of your paid social media campaigns depends heavily on the quality of your ad copy and visuals. Compelling ad content captures attention, communicates your message effectively, and encourages users to take action.

Writing Effective Ad Copy

Ad copy is the text that accompanies your ad visuals. It should be clear, concise, and persuasive. Here are some tips for writing effective ad copy:

- **Focus on Benefits:** Highlight the benefits of your product or service rather than just the features. Explain how it solves a problem or improves the user's life.
- **Create a Sense of Urgency:** Use time-sensitive language like "limited time offer," "today only," or "while supplies last" to encourage immediate action.
- **Use Clear Calls to Action (CTAs):** Your CTA should clearly state what you want the user to do, such as "Shop Now," "Sign Up," or "Learn More." A strong CTA drives users toward the desired action.
- **Speak to Your Audience:** Tailor your language and tone to resonate with your target audience. Use language that reflects their values, needs, and desires.
- **Keep It Short:** Social media users have limited attention spans, so keep your ad copy short and to the point. Aim for a clear and compelling message in just a few words.

Designing Eye-Catching Visuals

Visuals are the first thing users notice about your ad, so they need to be eye-catching and relevant. Here's how to create effective ad visuals:

-

High-Quality Images and Videos: Use high-resolution images and videos that are visually appealing and aligned with your brand's aesthetic. Avoid using stock photos that look generic or impersonal.

- **Consistent Branding:** Incorporate your brand's colors, fonts, and logo into your ad visuals to create a cohesive brand identity. Consistent branding helps build recognition and trust.

- **Focus on the Product:** If you're promoting a product, make sure it's the focal point of your visual. Show the product in use or highlight its key features.

- **Use Contrast and Color:** High contrast and bold colors can help your ad stand out in crowded social media feeds. Experiment with different color combinations to see what catches your audience's eye.

- **Keep It Simple:** Avoid cluttered designs with too much text or too many elements. A clean, simple design with a clear message is more likely to capture attention and drive action.

Ad Formats and Placement

Different platforms and ad formats require different design approaches. For example, Instagram Stories ads should be vertical and full-screen, while Facebook carousel ads allow for multiple images or videos in a single ad unit. Make sure your visuals are optimized for the specific format and placement you're using.

Analyzing Ad Performance and ROI

Measuring the success of your paid social media campaigns is essential to understanding what's working and what needs improvement. By analyzing key metrics and calculating your return on investment (ROI), you can refine your strategy and optimize future campaigns.

Key Metrics to Track

Different platforms offer various metrics to track the performance of your ads. Some of the most important metrics include:

- **Impressions:** The number of times your ad was displayed. High impressions indicate that your ad is being seen, but it doesn't necessarily mean users are engaging with it.
- **Click-Through Rate (CTR):** The percentage of users who clicked on your ad after seeing it. A high CTR indicates that your ad is compelling and relevant to your audience.
- **Conversion Rate:** The percentage of users who completed a desired action (e.g., making a purchase, signing up for a newsletter) after clicking on your ad. This is a key metric for measuring the effectiveness of your ad in driving results.
- **Cost Per Click (CPC):** The average amount you pay for each click on your ad. Lowering your CPC while maintaining or increasing your CTR can help you get more value from your ad spend.
- **Cost Per Conversion:** The average amount you pay for each conversion. This metric is crucial for understanding the cost-effectiveness of your campaign.
- **Return on Ad Spend (ROAS):** The revenue generated from your ad campaign divided by the cost of the

campaign. A ROAS greater than 1 indicates that your campaign is profitable.

Using Analytics Tools

Most social media platforms offer built-in analytics tools to help you track and analyze your ad performance. These tools provide detailed reports on key metrics and allow you to break down performance by audience segment, placement, and other factors.

- **Facebook Ads Manager:** Offers comprehensive reporting on ad performance, including audience insights, ad delivery, and conversion tracking.
- **Google Analytics:** Can be integrated with your social media campaigns to track traffic, conversions, and user behavior on your website.
- **LinkedIn Campaign Manager:** Provides insights into the performance of your LinkedIn ads, including engagement, clicks, and conversions.

Refining Your Strategy

Analyzing your ad performance is not just about measuring success—it's about learning and improving. Use the insights you gain to refine your targeting, adjust your ad copy and visuals, and optimize your bidding strategy. Regularly review your campaigns and make data-driven decisions to enhance your results.

Calculating ROI

To calculate the ROI of your social media advertising, use the following formula:

$$\text{ROI} = \frac{\text{Net Profit}}{\text{Total Ad Spend}} \times 100$$

For example, if your campaign generated $5,000 in revenue and your total ad spend was $1,000, your ROI would be:

$$\text{ROI} = \frac{5000 - 1000}{1000} \times 100 = 400\%$$

A positive ROI indicates that your campaign is profitable, while a negative ROI suggests that adjustments are needed.

In this chapter, you've learned about the fundamentals of paid social media advertising, how to budget and manage your ad spend, crafting compelling ad copy and visuals, and analyzing ad performance to maximize ROI. By applying these strategies, you can create effective and profitable ad campaigns that drive results and contribute to your overall business goals.

Chapter 6: Analytics and Measuring Success

Understanding and leveraging analytics is crucial for the success of any social media strategy. By tracking key metrics, using the right tools, and interpreting audience insights, you can make data-driven decisions that enhance your campaigns and achieve your goals. In this chapter, we'll explore the key metrics to track on each platform, the best tools for social media analytics, how to understand audience insights, and how to adjust your strategies based on the data you collect.

Key Metrics to Track on Each Platform

Each social media platform offers a variety of metrics that help you evaluate the performance of your content and campaigns. While the specific metrics may vary by platform, there are some common key performance indicators (KPIs) that you should monitor.

Facebook

- **Reach:** The number of unique users who saw your content. A high reach indicates that your content is visible to a large audience.
- **Engagement Rate:** The percentage of people who engaged with your content (likes, comments, shares) out of the total number of people who saw it. A higher engagement rate suggests that your content resonates with your audience.
- **Click-Through Rate (CTR):** The percentage of users who clicked on a link in your post or ad. A high CTR indicates that your content is compelling and encourages users to take action.

- **Conversion Rate:** The percentage of users who completed a desired action (e.g., filling out a form, making a purchase) after clicking on your content. This metric is crucial for evaluating the effectiveness of your content in driving results.

Instagram

- **Follower Growth:** The number of new followers gained over a specific period. Steady growth indicates increasing interest in your brand.
- **Engagement Rate per Post:** The level of interaction (likes, comments, shares) your posts receive relative to your follower count. This helps gauge how well your content resonates with your audience.
- **Story Views:** The number of times your Instagram Stories are viewed. Tracking which stories perform best can help you refine your content strategy.
- **Hashtag Performance:** The effectiveness of the hashtags you use in terms of reach and engagement. This can inform your future hashtag strategy.

Twitter (X)

- **Impressions:** The number of times your tweets appear in users' timelines. A higher number of impressions suggests greater visibility.
- **Engagement Rate:** The ratio of engagements (likes, retweets, replies) to the total number of impressions. A high engagement rate indicates that your tweets are interesting and relevant to your audience.

- **Mentions:** The number of times your brand is mentioned by other users. This helps measure brand awareness and sentiment.
- **Top Tweets:** Identifying which tweets generated the most engagement can help you understand what content resonates with your audience.

LinkedIn

- **Profile Views:** The number of times your LinkedIn profile is viewed. This is a good indicator of personal brand awareness and interest.
- **Post Engagement:** The number of likes, shares, and comments on your posts. High engagement suggests your content is valuable to your professional network.
- **Click-Through Rate (CTR):** The percentage of users who clicked on links in your posts or ads. This helps measure how effectively your content drives traffic.
- **InMail Response Rate:** The percentage of InMail messages that receive a reply. A high response rate indicates that your messages are relevant and engaging.

TikTok

- **Video Views:** The total number of views your videos receive. This metric indicates the reach and popularity of your content.
- **Engagement Rate:** The level of interaction (likes, comments, shares) relative to the number of views. A

higher engagement rate suggests that your content is resonating with viewers.

- **Follower Growth:** The rate at which you are gaining new followers. Consistent growth indicates increasing interest in your content.

- **Hashtag Challenges:** The number of users participating in your branded hashtag challenges. This is a key indicator of how well your brand is engaging the TikTok community.

Pinterest

- **Pin Impressions:** The number of times your pins are shown in users' feeds. High impressions indicate that your content is reaching a broad audience.

- **Saves (Repins):** The number of times users save your pins to their boards. Saves are a strong indicator of content relevance and value.

- **Clicks:** The number of clicks your pins receive, directing users to your website or landing page. High click numbers indicate effective calls to action and engaging content.

- **Engagement Rate:** The level of interaction (saves, comments, shares) relative to the number of impressions. A higher engagement rate indicates that your content is compelling to your audience.

Tools for Social Media Analytics

Tracking and analyzing social media metrics can be overwhelming without the right tools. Fortunately, there are several powerful analytics tools available that can help you gather data, generate reports, and gain insights into your social media performance.

Native Analytics Tools

Most social media platforms offer built-in analytics tools that provide a wealth of data about your content and audience. Here are some of the most commonly used native tools:

- **Facebook Insights:** Provides detailed metrics on page performance, post engagement, audience demographics, and more.
- **Instagram Insights:** Offers data on follower demographics, post and story performance, and engagement rates.
- **Twitter Analytics:** Tracks tweet impressions, engagement, follower growth, and top-performing content.
- **LinkedIn Analytics:** Provides insights into post performance, follower demographics, and engagement.
- **TikTok Analytics:** Tracks video views, follower growth, engagement, and trending content.
- **Pinterest Analytics:** Offers data on pin performance, audience insights, and website traffic generated from Pinterest.

Third-Party Analytics Tools

In addition to native tools, there are several third-party analytics platforms that offer more advanced features and the ability to track performance across multiple social media channels:

-

Google Analytics: While primarily a web analytics tool, Google Analytics can track social media traffic, conversions, and user behavior on your website.

-

Hootsuite Analytics: Provides detailed reports on social media performance across multiple platforms, with customizable dashboards and automated reporting.

-

Sprout Social: Offers in-depth analytics and reporting, along with features for social listening, engagement tracking, and audience analysis.

-

Buffer Analyze: Focuses on social media performance metrics, with easy-to-understand reports and recommendations for improving engagement.

-

Socialbakers: Provides comprehensive social media analytics, including competitive benchmarking, audience analysis, and content performance tracking.

Social Listening Tools

Social listening tools monitor online conversations about your brand, industry, or competitors. These tools help you understand brand sentiment, identify emerging trends, and respond to customer feedback:

-

Brandwatch: A powerful social listening platform that tracks brand mentions, sentiment, and industry trends across various social media platforms.

-

Mention: Monitors mentions of your brand, products, or competitors, allowing you to stay on top of online conversations.

-

BuzzSumo: Identifies popular content and influencers in your industry, helping you refine your content strategy based on what's trending.

Understanding Audience Insights

Audience insights go beyond basic demographics and tell you how your audience behaves, what they value, and how they interact with your content. Understanding these insights is crucial for tailoring your social media strategy to meet the needs and preferences of your audience.

Demographics

Demographics provide basic information about your audience, such as age, gender, location, language, and education level. This data helps you understand who your audience is and how to target your content effectively.

- **Age and Gender:** Knowing the age and gender distribution of your audience allows you to create content that resonates with their specific needs and interests.
- **Location:** Understanding where your audience is located helps you tailor your content to different regions and time zones, and informs your advertising targeting strategies.
- **Language:** If your audience is multilingual, consider creating content in multiple languages to reach a broader audience.

Interests and Behaviors

Interests and behaviors provide deeper insights into what your audience cares about and how they interact with your content:

- **Content Preferences:** Analyze which types of content (e.g., videos, articles, infographics) generate the most engagement. This can help you focus your efforts on the content formats that resonate best with your audience.
- **Activity Patterns:** Understanding when your audience is most active on social media allows you to schedule posts for maximum visibility and engagement.
- **Engagement Behavior:** Track how your audience interacts with your content, including likes, comments, shares, and clicks. High engagement indicates that your content is relevant and valuable to your audience.

Sentiment Analysis

Sentiment analysis evaluates the tone and emotion behind social media mentions and comments about your brand. Understanding sentiment helps you gauge public perception and respond appropriately:

- **Positive Sentiment:** Indicates that your audience is happy with your brand, products, or content. Leverage positive sentiment by amplifying these mentions and engaging with your satisfied customers.
- **Negative Sentiment:** Highlights areas of concern or dissatisfaction. Use this feedback to address issues, improve your products or services, and enhance customer experience.
- **Neutral Sentiment:** Indicates a lack of strong emotion. Consider ways to create more engaging content or interactions that elicit stronger emotional responses.

Adjusting Strategies Based on Data

Collecting and analyzing data is only the first step. The true value of social media analytics lies in using the insights you gain to refine and optimize your strategies. Here's how to adjust your social media strategy based on data:

Identify What's Working

Regularly review your top-performing content and campaigns to identify what's working well. Look for patterns in the types of content, topics, and formats that generate the most engagement, traffic, and conversions. Use these insights to replicate success in future campaigns.

- **Content Optimization:** Focus on creating more content similar to your top performers. For example, if videos consistently receive higher engagement than images, consider increasing your video output.
- **Audience Segmentation:** Analyze which segments of your audience are most responsive to your content. Tailor your messaging and content strategy to better serve these segments.

Address Underperforming Areas

Identify areas where your content or campaigns are underperforming and take action to address them. Low engagement, high bounce rates, or poor conversion rates indicate that adjustments are needed:

-

Revise Ad Copy or Visuals: If an ad is not performing well, consider revising the copy or visuals to better capture attention and communicate value.

- **Adjust Targeting:** If your content isn't resonating with your audience, revisit your targeting criteria. Ensure that you're reaching the right people with the right message.

- **Experiment with Timing:** If your posts aren't getting enough engagement, experiment with posting at different times of the day or week to find the optimal schedule.

A/B Testing and Iteration

A/B testing involves creating two or more versions of a piece of content or an ad and comparing their performance. This method allows you to test different variables, such as headlines, images, CTAs, or targeting options, to determine which version performs best.

- **Test One Variable at a Time:** To get clear results, focus on testing one variable at a time. For example, test two different headlines with the same image to see which one drives more clicks.

- **Iterate Based on Results:** Use the results of your A/B tests to inform future content and campaign decisions. Continuously iterate and optimize your strategy based on what works best.

Set New Goals Based on Insights

As you gather more data, your social media strategy should evolve. Use your insights to set new, more refined goals that reflect your current performance and future ambitions:

- **Refine Your KPIs:** Based on your analytics, adjust your key performance indicators to focus on the metrics that matter most to your business objectives.
- **Scale Successful Strategies:** If a particular strategy is working well, consider scaling it. For example, if a certain type of content consistently drives high engagement, allocate more resources to producing that content.
- **Address Emerging Trends:** Stay agile and responsive to emerging trends and changes in audience behavior. Adjust your strategy to take advantage of new opportunities or address potential challenges.

In this chapter, you've learned how to track key metrics on each platform, use tools for social media analytics, understand audience insights, and adjust your strategies based on data. By leveraging these practices, you can continuously optimize your social media efforts, improve your results, and achieve long-term success in your marketing endeavors.

Chapter 7: Managing Your Online Reputation

Your online reputation is one of your most valuable assets. In the age of social media, where information spreads rapidly, managing your reputation requires vigilance, strategy, and a proactive approach. This chapter will guide you through the essentials of handling negative feedback and trolls, building and maintaining brand trust, and effectively managing crises on social media.

Handling Negative Feedback and Trolls

Negative feedback and online trolls are inevitable on social media. How you handle these situations can significantly impact your brand's reputation. Addressing criticism with professionalism and empathy can turn a negative situation into an opportunity to strengthen your brand.

Responding to Negative Feedback

When receiving negative feedback, it's essential to respond thoughtfully and promptly. Ignoring complaints can lead to more frustration, while a well-crafted response can demonstrate your commitment to customer satisfaction.

- **Acknowledge the Issue:** Start by acknowledging the customer's concern. A simple acknowledgment shows that you're listening and taking their feedback seriously.
- **Apologize Sincerely:** If the complaint is valid, offer a sincere apology. Avoid making excuses and instead focus on how you can resolve the issue.
-

- **Offer a Solution:** Provide a clear solution or next steps to address the problem. This could involve offering a refund, replacing a product, or taking corrective action.
- **Take the Conversation Offline:** If the issue is complex or requires detailed discussion, invite the customer to continue the conversation privately via direct message, email, or phone. This allows you to resolve the matter more effectively and reduces public exposure.
- **Follow Up:** After resolving the issue, follow up with the customer to ensure they're satisfied with the outcome. A positive resolution can turn a dissatisfied customer into a loyal one.

Dealing with Trolls

Trolls are individuals who post inflammatory or off-topic comments with the intent to provoke others. Unlike genuine negative feedback, trolls are often not looking for resolution but rather to cause disruption. Here's how to handle trolls effectively:

- **Don't Feed the Trolls:** Avoid engaging with trolls, as responding can escalate the situation. Trolls thrive on attention, so the best course of action is often to ignore them.
- **Moderate Comments:** Use moderation tools to filter out inappropriate or harmful comments. Most social media platforms offer features to block or hide comments that contain certain keywords.
- **Block or Ban:** If a troll continues to disrupt your page or posts offensive content, consider blocking or banning them from your account. This prevents them from posting further comments.

- **Report Abuse:** If a troll is engaging in harassment, hate speech, or other violations of platform policies, report them to the platform's support team.

Turning Negative Feedback into Positive Outcomes

Not all negative feedback is detrimental. Constructive criticism can provide valuable insights into areas where your brand can improve. By addressing concerns and making improvements based on feedback, you can enhance your products, services, and overall customer experience.

- **Analyze Patterns:** Look for recurring themes in negative feedback to identify underlying issues. This could point to a larger problem that needs addressing, such as product quality or customer service.
- **Incorporate Feedback:** Use constructive criticism to inform changes or updates to your offerings. Communicate these improvements to your audience to show that you value their input.
- **Showcase Resolutions:** Share success stories where you've resolved customer issues publicly. This demonstrates transparency and your commitment to customer satisfaction.

Building and Maintaining Brand Trust

Trust is the foundation of any successful brand. In the digital age, where information (and misinformation) spreads quickly, maintaining trust requires consistent effort, transparency, and a customer-centric approach.

Transparency and Honesty

Transparency is key to building and maintaining trust with your audience. Being open about your business practices, product limitations, and even mistakes can enhance your credibility.

- **Communicate Clearly:** Ensure that your messaging is clear, honest, and free of misleading claims. Overpromising and underdelivering can quickly erode trust.
- **Admit Mistakes:** If your brand makes a mistake, own up to it. Apologize sincerely, explain what went wrong, and outline the steps you're taking to prevent it from happening again. This can turn a negative situation into an opportunity to build trust.
- **Share Behind-the-Scenes Content:** Giving your audience a glimpse behind the scenes can humanize your brand and build a deeper connection. Whether it's showcasing your team, explaining your production process, or sharing your brand's values, transparency fosters trust.

Consistency in Messaging and Actions

Consistency in your messaging and actions reinforces your brand's reliability. Inconsistencies, on the other hand, can confuse your audience and damage your reputation.

- **Align Messaging Across Channels:** Ensure that your messaging is consistent across all platforms, from social media and email to your website and customer service.

This consistency reinforces your brand identity and builds trust.

- **Deliver on Promises:** Whether it's product quality, delivery times, or customer support, consistently delivering on your promises is essential for maintaining trust. If you say you'll do something, make sure you follow through.

- **Engage Authentically:** Engage with your audience in a genuine and authentic manner. Avoid canned responses and take the time to personalize your interactions. Authenticity is key to building long-term relationships.

Customer-Centric Approach

A customer-centric approach puts the needs and preferences of your customers at the forefront of your business strategy. By prioritizing customer satisfaction, you can build a loyal following and maintain trust over time.

- **Listen to Your Customers:** Regularly solicit feedback from your customers through surveys, social media, and direct communication. Listening to your customers helps you understand their needs and address their concerns.

- **Act on Feedback:** Use customer feedback to make meaningful improvements to your products, services, and overall customer experience. Demonstrating that you value and act on feedback builds trust.

- **Reward Loyalty:** Show appreciation for your loyal customers by offering exclusive deals, early access to new products, or personalized experiences. Loyalty programs and special offers can help reinforce positive relationships.

Crisis Management on Social Media

Even with the best strategies in place, crises can happen. Whether it's a product recall, a PR disaster, or a social media blunder, how you handle a crisis can make or break your brand's reputation. Effective crisis management involves preparation, swift action, and clear communication.

Preparing for a Crisis

Preparation is key to effective crisis management. Having a plan in place allows you to respond quickly and effectively when a crisis occurs.

- **Create a Crisis Management Plan:** Develop a comprehensive crisis management plan that outlines the steps to take in various types of crises. Include roles and responsibilities, communication protocols, and approval processes.
- **Assemble a Crisis Response Team:** Designate a crisis response team that includes members from key departments such as PR, social media, customer service, and legal. This team should be trained to handle crises and make decisions under pressure.
- **Monitor Social Media:** Use social listening tools to monitor social media for early warning signs of a crisis. Identifying potential issues early allows you to address them before they escalate.

Responding to a Crisis

When a crisis occurs, how you respond is critical. Swift, transparent, and empathetic communication can help mitigate damage and begin the process of rebuilding trust.

- **Act Quickly:** Time is of the essence in a crisis. Respond as quickly as possible to acknowledge the situation and inform your audience that you're addressing it.
- **Be Transparent:** Provide clear and accurate information about the crisis. Explain what happened, how it affects your customers, and what steps you're taking to resolve the issue.
- **Show Empathy:** Demonstrate empathy and understanding for those affected by the crisis. Acknowledge the impact it may have on your customers and offer support or compensation where appropriate.
- **Use Multiple Channels:** Communicate across all relevant channels, including social media, email, your website, and traditional media. Consistent messaging across channels ensures that your audience receives accurate information.

Post-Crisis Recovery

After the immediate crisis has been managed, the focus should shift to recovery and rebuilding trust.

- **Follow Up:** Keep your audience informed about the steps you're taking to prevent a similar crisis from occurring in the future. Provide updates as necessary and be transparent about any changes you're making.
- **Evaluate Your Response:** Conduct a post-crisis analysis to evaluate your response. Identify what worked well and

what could be improved. Use these insights to refine your crisis management plan.

- **Rebuild Trust:** Rebuilding trust takes time. Continue to engage with your audience authentically and demonstrate your commitment to doing better. Highlight positive changes or improvements that have resulted from the crisis.

In this chapter, you've learned how to manage your online reputation by handling negative feedback and trolls, building and maintaining brand trust, and effectively managing crises on social media. By implementing these strategies, you can protect and enhance your brand's reputation, ensuring long-term success in the digital age.

Chapter 8: Advanced Strategies for Social Media Mastery

To truly master social media, you need to go beyond the basics and explore advanced strategies that can elevate your brand's presence and effectiveness. In this chapter, we'll delve into the power of video content, leveraging user-generated content, harnessing the potential of social media automation, and exploring new and emerging platforms. These strategies will help you stay ahead of the competition and maximize your impact in the ever-evolving social media landscape.

The Power of Video Content

Video content has become a dominant force in social media marketing. With its ability to engage, inform, and entertain, video is a powerful tool for capturing attention and driving action. As platforms like YouTube, Instagram, TikTok, and Facebook prioritize video content, mastering video marketing is essential for social media success.

Why Video Content is Essential

- **High Engagement:** Video content consistently outperforms other types of content in terms of engagement. Videos are more likely to be liked, shared, and commented on than text or image posts.
- **Increased Reach:** Social media algorithms often prioritize video content, making it more likely to appear in users' feeds and reach a broader audience.
-

- **Storytelling:** Video is an excellent medium for storytelling, allowing you to convey your brand's message in a dynamic and visually compelling way.

- **Versatility:** Videos can be used for a variety of purposes, including product demonstrations, tutorials, behind-the-scenes looks, customer testimonials, and more.

Types of Video Content to Consider

- **Live Video:** Live streaming on platforms like Facebook, Instagram, and YouTube allows you to interact with your audience in real-time. Use live video for Q&A sessions, product launches, or exclusive behind-the-scenes content.

- **Short-Form Video:** Platforms like TikTok and Instagram Reels have popularized short-form video content. These quick, engaging videos are perfect for capturing attention and participating in trending challenges or topics.

- **Long-Form Video:** Longer videos, such as those on YouTube or IGTV, are ideal for in-depth content like tutorials, interviews, or educational series. Long-form video allows you to provide more value and build a deeper connection with your audience.

- **Stories:** Stories on Instagram, Facebook, and Snapchat are temporary videos or images that disappear after 24 hours. Stories are perfect for sharing timely content, promoting limited-time offers, or giving your audience a behind-the-scenes look at your brand.

Best Practices for Creating Video Content

Capture Attention Quickly: The first few seconds of your video are crucial for capturing attention. Start with a strong hook to keep viewers engaged.

- **Keep It Short and Sweet:** While long-form videos have their place, shorter videos tend to perform better on social media. Aim for 15-60 seconds for most platforms, unless the content requires more depth.

- **Optimize for Mobile:** The majority of social media users access platforms via mobile devices. Ensure that your videos are optimized for mobile viewing, with clear visuals, large text, and vertical orientation when appropriate.

- **Include Captions:** Many users watch videos with the sound off, so adding captions ensures that your message is conveyed even without audio.

- **End with a Strong CTA:** Every video should have a clear call to action (CTA), whether it's asking viewers to visit your website, subscribe to your channel, or follow your profile.

Leveraging User-Generated Content

User-generated content (UGC) is any content created by your customers or followers rather than your brand. Leveraging UGC is an advanced strategy that not only saves time and resources but also builds trust and fosters community engagement.

Benefits of User-Generated Content

-

- **Authenticity:** UGC is seen as more authentic and trustworthy than brand-created content because it comes from real customers sharing their genuine experiences.
- **Increased Engagement:** UGC tends to generate higher engagement rates because it encourages participation from your audience and showcases real-life use cases of your products or services.
- **Cost-Effective:** By leveraging content created by your customers, you can save time and resources that would otherwise be spent on content creation.

How to Encourage User-Generated Content

- **Create Branded Hashtags:** Develop a unique, branded hashtag that your followers can use when sharing content related to your brand. Promote the hashtag in your posts, profile bio, and marketing materials to encourage its use.
- **Run Contests and Challenges:** Host contests or challenges that encourage your audience to create and share content featuring your products. Offer incentives such as prizes, discounts, or features on your brand's social media profiles.
- **Feature Customer Content:** Regularly feature UGC on your social media profiles, website, or email newsletters. This not only gives recognition to your customers but also encourages others to share their content in hopes of being featured.
- **Ask for Reviews and Testimonials:** Encourage satisfied customers to share reviews, testimonials, or unboxing videos. These types of UGC can be particularly effective in building trust with potential customers.

Best Practices for Using User-Generated Content

- **Get Permission:** Always ask for permission before reposting or sharing UGC. This shows respect for your customers and avoids any potential legal issues.
- **Give Credit:** When sharing UGC, always credit the original creator by tagging their profile or mentioning their username in your post.
- **Maintain Quality:** While UGC is valuable, ensure that the content aligns with your brand's quality standards. If necessary, you can edit or enhance UGC to better fit your brand's aesthetic.
- **Incorporate UGC into Paid Campaigns:** UGC can be incredibly effective in paid social media campaigns. Consider using UGC in your ads to add authenticity and social proof to your marketing efforts.

Harnessing the Potential of Social Media Automation

Social media automation involves using tools and software to manage, schedule, and analyze your social media activities. When used correctly, automation can save time, improve consistency, and enhance the effectiveness of your social media strategy.

Benefits of Social Media Automation

- **Time Efficiency:** Automation tools allow you to schedule posts in advance, freeing up time to focus on other aspects of your business.

- **Consistency:** Regular posting is key to maintaining engagement, and automation ensures that your content is published consistently, even when you're busy.

- **Enhanced Analytics:** Many automation tools come with advanced analytics features that provide insights into your content performance and audience behavior, helping you make data-driven decisions.

Tools for Social Media Automation

- **Hootsuite:** A comprehensive social media management tool that allows you to schedule posts, monitor conversations, and analyze performance across multiple platforms.

- **Buffer:** A user-friendly tool for scheduling posts, tracking engagement, and analyzing the effectiveness of your content.

- **Sprout Social:** A robust platform that offers social media scheduling, analytics, and engagement features, along with powerful social listening tools.

- **Later:** A visual content calendar and scheduling tool, particularly popular for Instagram, that allows you to plan and schedule posts visually.

- **Zapier:** An automation tool that connects different apps and automates tasks, such as posting to social media when a new blog post is published.

Best Practices for Social Media Automation

- **Maintain Authenticity:** While automation can handle many tasks, it's important to maintain a human touch.

Engage with your audience directly by responding to comments and messages in real-time.

- **Monitor and Adjust:** Regularly review your automated posts and adjust your strategy based on performance. Automation should complement, not replace, a thoughtful content strategy.

- **Avoid Over-Automation:** While automation is a powerful tool, avoid over-relying on it. Automated posts should still be relevant, timely, and tailored to your audience's preferences.

- **Use Automation for Repetitive Tasks:** Focus your automation efforts on repetitive tasks like scheduling posts, curating content, and generating reports. This frees up time for more creative and strategic work.

Exploring New and Emerging Platforms

The social media landscape is constantly evolving, with new platforms emerging regularly. Staying ahead of the curve by exploring and experimenting with new platforms can give your brand a competitive edge and help you reach new audiences.

Why Explore New Platforms?

- **Early Adopter Advantage:** Being an early adopter of a new platform allows you to establish a presence before the platform becomes saturated. Early adopters often benefit from lower competition and higher organic reach.

- **Reaching Niche Audiences:** Emerging platforms often cater to specific niches or demographics. By joining these platforms, you can connect with niche audiences that may be more difficult to reach on mainstream platforms.

-

Staying Relevant: As social media trends evolve, keeping up with new platforms ensures that your brand remains relevant and adapts to changing user behaviors.

Popular Emerging Platforms to Consider

-

Clubhouse: An audio-based social networking app that allows users to join virtual rooms and participate in live discussions on various topics. Ideal for thought leadership, networking, and engaging in real-time conversations.

-

TikTok: While no longer "new," TikTok continues to grow rapidly, especially among younger audiences. Its short-form video format and algorithm-driven content discovery make it a powerful platform for creative, viral content.

-

Discord: Originally a platform for gamers, Discord has expanded into a community-building tool for various interests and industries. Brands can create their own servers to host discussions, share content, and engage with their audience in a more intimate setting.

-

BeReal: A relatively new social media app that prompts users to share a photo at a random time each day, capturing a more authentic, unfiltered moment. BeReal's focus on authenticity appeals to users looking for more genuine connections.

-

Twitch: A live streaming platform primarily known for gaming but increasingly used for other content categories like music, art, and talk shows. Twitch offers opportunities for live interaction and building a dedicated community.

How to Approach New Platforms

- **Start Small:** When exploring a new platform, start with a small-scale experiment. Test different types of content, engage with users, and assess whether the platform aligns with your brand's goals.

- **Monitor Trends:** Keep an eye on social media trends and user behavior on emerging platforms. Look for signs that a platform is gaining traction or that your target audience is migrating to it.

- **Be Flexible:** Be prepared to adapt your strategy based on the unique features and culture of each platform. What works on Instagram may not work on TikTok, so tailor your approach accordingly.

- **Evaluate ROI:** After experimenting with a new platform, evaluate the return on investment (ROI). Consider the time and resources required versus the potential benefits, and decide whether to continue or scale back your efforts.

In this chapter, you've explored advanced strategies for social media mastery, including the power of video content, leveraging user-generated content, harnessing social media automation, and exploring new and emerging platforms. By incorporating these strategies into your social media plan, you can elevate your brand's presence, stay ahead of trends, and maximize your impact in the ever-changing world of social media.

Chapter 9: Integrating Social Media with Other Marketing Channels

Integrating social media with other marketing channels is essential for creating a cohesive and effective marketing strategy. By aligning your social media efforts with email marketing, SEO, and other channels, you can enhance your brand's reach, improve customer engagement, and drive better results. In this chapter, we'll explore the role of social media in omnichannel marketing, cross-promotion strategies, how to integrate social media with email marketing, and the synergy between social media and SEO.

The Role of Social Media in Omnichannel Marketing

Omnichannel marketing is an approach that ensures a seamless and consistent customer experience across all touchpoints, whether online or offline. Social media plays a critical role in an omnichannel strategy by connecting various channels and providing a platform for real-time engagement with customers.

Why Omnichannel Marketing Matters

- **Consistency:** Omnichannel marketing ensures that your brand messaging is consistent across all channels, which helps build trust and brand recognition.
- **Customer Experience:** By integrating all channels, you provide a smoother and more personalized customer journey, improving customer satisfaction and loyalty.
- **Data Integration:** Omnichannel strategies allow you to collect and analyze data from multiple touchpoints, giving

you a comprehensive view of customer behavior and preferences.

Social Media as a Central Hub

Social media often serves as the central hub in an omnichannel marketing strategy because of its ability to reach a wide audience and facilitate two-way communication. Here's how social media integrates with other channels:

- **Customer Service:** Social media is a key channel for customer service, allowing you to respond to inquiries, address issues, and engage with customers in real-time.
- **Content Distribution:** Social media platforms are ideal for distributing content, from blog posts and videos to product announcements and promotions. This content can then drive traffic to other channels like your website or email list.
- **Feedback Loop:** Social media provides immediate feedback from customers, which can inform your strategies on other channels, such as product development, email campaigns, or website improvements.

Cross-Promotion Strategies

Cross-promotion involves leveraging multiple marketing channels to promote content, products, or campaigns, creating a more comprehensive and impactful marketing effort. By cross-promoting on social media and other channels, you can increase visibility, drive traffic, and reinforce your messaging.

Cross-Promoting Across Social Media Platforms

Each social media platform has its unique strengths, and cross-promoting content across these platforms can help you reach different segments of your audience:

- **Teasers and Trailers:** Use Instagram Stories or Twitter to tease longer-form content, such as YouTube videos or blog posts. This creates anticipation and drives traffic to the full content.
- **Hashtags and Trends:** Leverage popular hashtags or trends on platforms like Twitter and Instagram to amplify your reach. Then, direct users to related content on your other platforms.
- **Repurposing Content:** Adapt content from one platform to suit another. For example, turn a LinkedIn article into an infographic for Pinterest or a short video clip for TikTok.

Cross-Promoting with Email Marketing

Email marketing is one of the most effective channels for nurturing leads and driving conversions. By integrating email with social media, you can enhance both channels' effectiveness:

- **Social Media in Email Campaigns:** Include social media icons and CTAs in your emails to encourage subscribers to follow your social profiles. You can also feature social media content, such as user-generated content or recent posts, in your newsletters.
- **Email List Building on Social Media:** Use social media ads and organic posts to drive traffic to landing pages where users can sign up for your email list. Offer incentives, such as exclusive content or discounts, to encourage sign-ups.

- **Social Proof in Emails:** Incorporate social proof, such as testimonials, reviews, or user-generated content from your social media channels, into your email campaigns to build credibility and trust.

Cross-Promoting with Offline Channels

Offline channels, such as in-store promotions, events, or print media, can also be integrated with social media:

- **Events and Social Media:** Promote offline events on social media before, during, and after the event. Encourage attendees to share their experiences on social media using a specific hashtag, and consider live-streaming parts of the event to reach a broader audience.
- **QR Codes:** Use QR codes in print ads, direct mail, or in-store displays that link to your social media profiles, website, or a specific campaign landing page.
- **Branded Merchandise:** Encourage customers to share photos of themselves using or wearing branded merchandise on social media. Feature this user-generated content on your profiles to build community and brand loyalty.

Email Marketing and Social Media

Email marketing and social media are powerful channels on their own, but when combined, they can create a synergistic effect that enhances both strategies. Integrating email marketing with social media allows you to extend your reach, deepen customer relationships, and drive conversions.

Building Your Email List through Social Media

Growing your email list is essential for maintaining a direct line of communication with your audience. Social media is an effective tool for driving email sign-ups:

- **Lead Generation Ads:** Use Facebook and Instagram lead generation ads to capture email addresses directly from social media. These ads allow users to sign up for your email list without leaving the platform.
- **Exclusive Offers:** Promote exclusive offers, such as discounts, free trials, or downloadable content, on social media to incentivize followers to join your email list.
- **Contests and Giveaways:** Host contests or giveaways on social media that require users to enter their email addresses to participate. This not only grows your email list but also boosts engagement on your social profiles.

Enhancing Email Campaigns with Social Media

Integrating social media into your email campaigns can increase engagement and drive more traffic to your social profiles:

- **Social Sharing Buttons:** Include social sharing buttons in your emails to encourage subscribers to share your content with their networks. This can help expand your reach and attract new followers.
- **Highlight Social Content:** Feature your top-performing social media posts, user-generated content, or social proof in your emails. This not only provides additional content

for your emails but also reinforces your social media presence.

- **Segmented Social Campaigns:** Use insights from your email marketing campaigns to create targeted social media ads. For example, you can retarget email subscribers who didn't open a specific campaign with a related social media ad.

Retargeting Email Subscribers on Social Media

Retargeting is a powerful strategy that involves showing ads to users who have already interacted with your brand, such as visiting your website or engaging with your emails:

- **Custom Audiences:** Create custom audiences on platforms like Facebook and Instagram using your email list. This allows you to show targeted ads to people who have already shown interest in your brand, increasing the likelihood of conversions.

- **Dynamic Retargeting:** Use dynamic retargeting ads to show personalized content or products to users based on their previous interactions with your emails. For example, if a subscriber clicked on a specific product in your email, you can retarget them with an ad for that product.

Integrating Social Media with SEO

Search engine optimization (SEO) and social media marketing are often viewed as separate strategies, but integrating them can enhance your online visibility and drive more organic traffic to your website. By aligning your social media and SEO efforts, you can improve your search rankings and increase brand awareness.

The Relationship Between Social Media and SEO

While social media activity itself does not directly impact search rankings, it can indirectly influence SEO in several ways:

- **Increased Website Traffic:** Social media drives traffic to your website, which can improve your site's engagement metrics (e.g., time on site, pages per session), signaling to search engines that your site is valuable to users.
- **Content Amplification:** Sharing content on social media increases its visibility and the likelihood that it will be linked to by other websites, which is a key factor in SEO.
- **Brand Awareness and Searches:** A strong social media presence can increase brand awareness, leading to more branded searches on search engines, which can positively impact your rankings.

Optimizing Social Media Profiles for SEO

Your social media profiles can contribute to your overall SEO strategy by appearing in search results and driving traffic to your website:

- **Consistent Branding:** Ensure that your brand name, logo, and messaging are consistent across all social media profiles. This consistency reinforces your brand identity and helps with search engine recognition.
- **Keyword Optimization:** Use relevant keywords in your social media bios, descriptions, and posts. This can

improve the discoverability of your profiles both on social media platforms and in search engine results.

- **Link Building:** Include links to your website, blog, and other key pages in your social media profiles. These links drive traffic and can also be valuable for SEO if they generate backlinks from other websites.

Creating SEO-Friendly Content for Social Media

Content that performs well on social media can also benefit your SEO efforts, especially when it drives traffic to your website:

- **Shareable Content:** Create content that is highly shareable and encourages engagement, such as infographics, listicles, or how-to guides. The more your content is shared, the more visibility it gains, increasing the chances of earning backlinks.

- **Use of Hashtags and Keywords:** Incorporate relevant hashtags and keywords into your social media posts to increase their visibility and discoverability. This can lead to higher engagement and more website traffic.

- **Cross-Promote Blog Content:** Promote your blog posts on social media to drive traffic and encourage shares. Make sure your blog content is optimized for SEO with relevant keywords, meta descriptions, and internal links.

Leveraging Social Media for Link Building

Link building is a critical component of SEO, and social media can play a role in generating high-quality backlinks:

-

- **Content Distribution:** Share your content across social media platforms to increase its reach and the likelihood of being linked to by other websites.
- **Influencer Outreach:** Collaborate with influencers or industry experts who can share your content with their followers. This can lead to additional exposure and potential backlinks.
- **Engage with Industry Communities:** Participate in industry-specific social media groups, forums, or communities. Sharing your content in these spaces can result in more links from reputable sources.

In this chapter, you've learned how to integrate social media with other marketing channels, including omnichannel marketing, cross-promotion strategies, email marketing, and SEO. By aligning your social media efforts with these channels, you can create a more cohesive and effective marketing strategy that drives better results and enhances your brand's overall visibility and impact.

Chapter 10: The Future of Social Media Marketing

As social media continues to evolve at a rapid pace, staying ahead of the curve is essential for brands looking to maintain a competitive edge. The future of social media marketing will be shaped by emerging trends, technological advancements, and changing consumer behaviors. In this chapter, we'll explore key trends to watch in social media, the impact of AI and machine learning, and how to prepare your brand for the future.

Trends to Watch in Social Media

Understanding and adapting to emerging trends is crucial for maintaining relevance and effectively engaging with your audience. Here are some of the most significant trends to watch in the coming years:

Short-Form Video Dominance

Short-form video content, popularized by platforms like TikTok, Instagram Reels, and YouTube Shorts, will continue to dominate social media. The bite-sized, engaging nature of short-form videos makes them highly effective for capturing attention and driving engagement.

-
    Increased Adoption by Brands: More brands will adopt short-form video as a core component of their content strategy. Expect to see creative, quick-hitting videos that convey brand messages, showcase products, or entertain audiences.
-

- **Integration Across Platforms:** Even platforms not traditionally known for video content, like LinkedIn, may integrate more short-form video features to keep up with consumer demand.

Social Commerce Growth

Social commerce, the integration of e-commerce and social media, is expected to grow significantly. Platforms like Instagram, Facebook, and Pinterest are enhancing their shopping features, making it easier for users to discover and purchase products directly from their feeds.

- **Seamless Shopping Experiences:** The line between social media and e-commerce will blur further, with platforms offering more seamless, in-app purchasing experiences.
- **Livestream Shopping:** Livestream shopping, already popular in markets like China, will gain traction globally. Brands will host live events where users can shop in real-time, creating a more interactive shopping experience.

Augmented Reality (AR) and Virtual Reality (VR) Integration

AR and VR technologies are becoming more accessible, and social media platforms are beginning to integrate these immersive experiences.

- **AR Filters and Lenses:** Expect to see more brands using AR filters and lenses on platforms like Instagram and Snapchat to create interactive and engaging content that users can personalize and share.
- **Virtual Brand Experiences:** VR will enable brands to create fully immersive virtual experiences, such as virtual

stores, events, or showrooms, where users can interact with products or brand representatives in a virtual environment.

The Rise of Niche Platforms

While major platforms like Facebook and Instagram will continue to dominate, niche platforms that cater to specific interests or communities will grow in popularity.

- **Community-Driven Platforms:** Platforms like Discord, which focus on community-building and niche interests, will attract more brands looking to engage with highly targeted audiences.

- **Privacy-Focused Social Media:** With growing concerns about privacy, platforms that prioritize user privacy and data security, such as Signal or MeWe, may see increased adoption.

Sustainability and Social Responsibility

Consumers are increasingly expecting brands to take a stand on social and environmental issues. Social media will play a key role in how brands communicate their values and sustainability efforts.

- **Purpose-Driven Campaigns:** Brands will focus on creating campaigns that highlight their commitment to sustainability, diversity, and social responsibility, resonating with consumers who prioritize these values.

- **Transparent Communication:** Transparency will be critical, as consumers demand more information about a brand's practices. Social media will be a primary channel for sharing this information.

The Impact of AI and Machine Learning on Social Media

Artificial intelligence (AI) and machine learning are transforming how brands approach social media marketing. From content creation to customer service, these technologies offer powerful tools for enhancing efficiency, personalization, and engagement.

AI-Driven Content Creation and Curation

AI is increasingly being used to assist with content creation and curation, helping brands produce and distribute content more effectively.

- **Automated Content Creation:** AI tools like natural language processing (NLP) and image recognition can generate written content, images, and videos automatically. While human creativity remains essential, AI can handle repetitive tasks and scale content production.

- **Personalized Content Recommendations:** Machine learning algorithms can analyze user behavior to recommend personalized content, ensuring that users see content that aligns with their interests, leading to higher engagement rates.

Enhanced Customer Service with AI

AI-powered chatbots and virtual assistants are becoming more sophisticated, providing faster and more personalized customer service on social media.

-

- **24/7 Availability:** Chatbots can handle customer inquiries at any time, providing instant responses and freeing up human agents for more complex issues.

- **Natural Language Processing:** Advanced NLP allows chatbots to understand and respond to customer inquiries more accurately, improving the overall customer experience.

Advanced Analytics and Insights

AI and machine learning are revolutionizing how brands analyze social media data, offering deeper insights and more accurate predictions.

- **Predictive Analytics:** AI can analyze historical data to predict future trends, helping brands anticipate changes in customer behavior and adjust their strategies accordingly.

- **Sentiment Analysis:** AI-powered sentiment analysis tools can automatically assess the tone of social media mentions and comments, allowing brands to gauge public sentiment and respond appropriately.

Ad Targeting and Optimization

AI is enhancing the effectiveness of social media advertising by improving targeting and optimization.

- **Dynamic Ad Targeting:** AI can analyze user data in real-time to dynamically adjust ad targeting, ensuring that ads are shown to the most relevant audience at the optimal time.

-

Automated A/B Testing: Machine learning algorithms can automatically conduct A/B tests on ad creatives, headlines, and targeting options, optimizing campaigns for better performance.

Preparing Your Brand for the Future

To stay competitive in the evolving social media landscape, brands must be proactive in adopting new technologies, experimenting with emerging trends, and adapting to changing consumer behaviors. Here's how to prepare your brand for the future:

Embrace Innovation

Staying ahead of the curve requires a willingness to embrace new technologies and platforms. Keep an eye on emerging trends and be open to experimenting with innovative strategies.

- **Experiment with New Formats:** Don't be afraid to test new content formats, such as AR filters, short-form videos, or livestreams. Experimentation allows you to discover what resonates with your audience and keeps your brand relevant.

- **Adopt AI and Automation:** Leverage AI and automation tools to streamline your social media processes, enhance personalization, and improve efficiency. Invest in technologies that can help you scale your efforts and stay competitive.

Focus on Authenticity and Transparency

As consumers become more discerning, authenticity and transparency will be key to building and maintaining trust.

- **Be Transparent:** Be open about your brand's values, practices, and challenges. Transparency builds trust and loyalty, especially when it comes to social and environmental issues.

- **Engage Authentically:** Focus on genuine engagement with your audience rather than overly polished or scripted content. Authenticity resonates more with consumers and fosters deeper connections.

Stay Agile and Adaptive

The social media landscape can change quickly, so it's important to stay agile and be ready to adapt your strategy as needed.

- **Monitor Trends Continuously:** Keep a close eye on industry trends, consumer behavior, and platform updates. Regularly review and adjust your social media strategy based on these insights.

- **Be Ready to Pivot:** If a strategy or platform isn't delivering the desired results, be prepared to pivot and try something new. Flexibility is crucial in a rapidly changing digital environment.

Invest in Continuous Learning

The future of social media marketing will be shaped by continuous learning and skill development. Invest in training and education to ensure your team stays at the forefront of industry advancements.

- **Stay Informed:** Follow industry blogs, attend webinars, and participate in online courses to stay up-to-date with the latest trends and best practices in social media marketing.

- **Encourage Skill Development:** Encourage your team to develop new skills, whether it's mastering AI tools, creating video content, or analyzing data. A well-rounded team will be better equipped to navigate the future of social media.

In this chapter, you've explored the future of social media marketing, including key trends to watch, the impact of AI and machine learning, and how to prepare your brand for what's ahead. By staying informed, embracing innovation, and remaining adaptable, you can position your brand for long-term success in the ever-evolving world of social media.

Conclusion

As you reach the end of this comprehensive guide to social media marketing, it's important to take a moment to reflect on the key strategies and insights you've gained. Social media is a powerful tool for building your brand and connecting with your audience, but success requires a strategic approach, ongoing effort, and a willingness to adapt to the ever-changing digital landscape.

Recap of Key Strategies

Throughout this book, we've explored a wide range of strategies designed to help you master social media marketing and build a successful online presence. Here's a quick recap of the most important takeaways:

- **Understanding Your Audience:** Everything starts with knowing your audience. By understanding their demographics, interests, and behaviors, you can create content that resonates and drives engagement.
- **Content Creation and Curation:** High-quality content is the foundation of social media success. Focus on creating valuable, engaging, and visually appealing content, while also curating relevant content that adds value to your audience.
- **Storytelling:** Use storytelling to connect with your audience on an emotional level. Whether through videos, posts, or user-generated content, telling a compelling story helps build brand loyalty.
- **Growing Your Audience:** Implement strategies like leveraging hashtags, engaging with followers,

collaborating with influencers, and running contests to organically grow your audience.

- **Paid Advertising:** Use paid social media advertising to reach specific target audiences, drive traffic, and increase conversions. Craft compelling ad copy and visuals, and continuously optimize your campaigns for better ROI.
- **Analytics and Measurement:** Track key metrics, use analytics tools to gain insights, and adjust your strategies based on data. Regularly monitor your performance to ensure you're meeting your goals.
- **Managing Your Reputation:** Handle negative feedback professionally, build and maintain brand trust, and be prepared to manage crises effectively on social media.
- **Advanced Strategies:** Stay ahead of the competition by leveraging video content, user-generated content, social media automation, and exploring new platforms.
- **Integration with Other Channels:** Integrate social media with email marketing, SEO, and other channels to create a cohesive and effective omnichannel marketing strategy.
-
  Preparing for the Future: Embrace innovation, focus on authenticity, stay agile, and invest in continuous learning to ensure your brand remains relevant and successful in the evolving social media landscape.

Next Steps for Your Social Media Journey

Now that you've equipped yourself with the knowledge and strategies needed to succeed in social media marketing, it's time to take action. Here are the next steps you should consider:

1. **Audit Your Current Social Media Presence:** Start by evaluating your current social media profiles, content, and performance. Identify areas for improvement and set clear goals for your social media strategy.
2. **Develop a Strategic Plan:** Based on the insights and strategies in this book, create a comprehensive social media plan that outlines your objectives, target audience, content strategy, posting schedule, and measurement criteria.
3. **Implement and Experiment:** Put your plan into action, but don't be afraid to experiment. Social media is dynamic, and what works today may not work tomorrow. Test different approaches, learn from your results, and be ready to pivot as needed.
4. **Engage and Build Relationships:** Focus on building genuine relationships with your audience. Engage with them authentically, respond to their feedback, and create a community around your brand.
5. **Monitor and Adjust:** Regularly monitor your performance using analytics tools, and be prepared to adjust your strategy based on the data. Stay informed about industry trends and be proactive in adapting to changes.
6. **Continue Learning:** Social media is constantly evolving, so commit to continuous learning. Stay updated on the latest trends, tools, and best practices to ensure your brand remains at the forefront of the digital landscape.

Final Thoughts on Building a Successful Brand Online

Building a successful brand online is a journey that requires dedication, creativity, and a deep understanding of your audience. Social media provides a unique opportunity to connect with people, tell your brand's story, and create meaningful relationships that drive long-term success.

Remember that success in social media marketing doesn't happen overnight. It's a process of trial and error, learning and adapting. But with the right strategies and a commitment to staying true to your brand's values, you can build a strong online presence that not only resonates with your audience but also drives tangible results for your business.

As you move forward in your social media journey, stay curious, stay innovative, and always keep your audience at the heart of everything you do. The digital world is full of opportunities—now it's your turn to seize them and build a brand that stands out in the crowded social media landscape.

Thank you for joining me on this journey through social media marketing mastery. I wish you all the best in your efforts to build and grow your brand online!

With this conclusion, your guide to social media marketing is complete. Now, it's time to put these strategies into practice and watch your brand thrive in the digital world.

Appendices

The appendices provide additional resources, definitions, templates, and real-world examples to help you further understand and implement the strategies discussed in this book. Whether you're new to social media marketing or a seasoned professional, these resources are designed to enhance your knowledge and support your efforts in building a successful brand online.

Glossary of Social Media Terms

Understanding social media jargon is essential for effective communication and strategy execution. Here's a glossary of common social media terms you're likely to encounter:

- **Algorithm:** A set of rules or calculations used by social media platforms to determine which content appears in users' feeds.
- **Analytics:** Data and metrics that provide insights into the performance of your social media content, campaigns, and overall presence.
- **Avatar:** A visual representation of a user or brand, often in the form of a profile picture or icon.
- **Bio:** A short description found on social media profiles that provides information about the user or brand.
- **Brand Advocate:** A customer or fan who actively promotes and supports your brand, often through word-of-mouth or social media mentions.
-

Click-Through Rate (CTR): The percentage of users who click on a link or call to action in a social media post or ad, relative to the number of impressions.

- **Content Curation:** The process of gathering, organizing, and sharing content created by others that is relevant to your audience.

- **Conversion Rate:** The percentage of users who complete a desired action (e.g., making a purchase, signing up for a newsletter) after interacting with your content or ad.

- **Engagement Rate:** A metric that measures the level of interaction (likes, comments, shares) your content receives relative to your follower count or impressions.

- **Follower:** A user who subscribes to your social media profile and receives your updates in their feed.

- **Hashtag:** A keyword or phrase preceded by the "#" symbol, used to categorize content and make it discoverable by users interested in that topic.

- **Impressions:** The number of times your content is displayed to users, regardless of whether it was clicked or engaged with.

- **Influencer:** An individual with a large following and the ability to influence the opinions and behaviors of their audience, often through social media.

- **Live Streaming:** Broadcasting live video content in real-time to your audience on social media platforms.

- **Organic Reach:** The number of people who see your content without paid promotion, typically through followers or shares.

- **Paid Reach:** The number of people who see your content as a result of paid advertising or promotion.
- **Retargeting:** A type of online advertising that targets users who have previously visited your website or interacted with your content.
- **Social Listening:** The practice of monitoring social media platforms for mentions of your brand, products, competitors, or industry to gain insights and respond appropriately.
- **User-Generated Content (UGC):** Content created by your customers or followers, often featuring your products or brand, that can be shared on your social media channels.
- **Vanity Metrics:** Metrics like likes, shares, and followers that may look impressive but don't necessarily indicate the effectiveness of your social media strategy in achieving business goals.
- **Viral Content:** Content that spreads rapidly across social media platforms, often due to its engaging, humorous, or relatable nature.

Recommended Tools and Resources

Here's a list of recommended tools and resources to help you manage, analyze, and optimize your social media efforts:

Social Media Management Tools

-

- **Hootsuite:** A comprehensive tool for managing multiple social media accounts, scheduling posts, and analyzing performance.
- **Buffer:** A user-friendly platform for scheduling social media posts, tracking engagement, and analyzing results.
- **Sprout Social:** An all-in-one social media management tool that includes publishing, engagement, and analytics features, along with social listening capabilities.
- **Later:** A visual content calendar and scheduling tool, especially popular for Instagram, that helps plan and schedule posts visually.
- **CoSchedule:** A marketing calendar that helps organize, schedule, and manage content across multiple social media channels.

Content Creation and Design Tools

- **Canva:** A graphic design tool with easy-to-use templates for creating social media posts, infographics, banners, and more.
- **Adobe Spark:** A suite of design tools for creating social media graphics, short videos, and web pages.
- **Piktochart:** A tool for creating visually appealing infographics, presentations, and social media content.
- **Animoto:** A video creation tool that allows you to create professional-quality videos for social media, complete with music, text, and effects.

Unsplash: A source of high-quality, royalty-free images that you can use in your social media posts and content.

Analytics and Reporting Tools

- **Google Analytics:** A powerful web analytics tool that tracks social media traffic, user behavior, and conversions on your website.
- **Socialbakers:** A social media analytics platform that offers insights into content performance, audience engagement, and competitive benchmarking.
- **HubSpot:** A marketing platform that includes social media analytics, allowing you to track performance and measure ROI.
- **Brandwatch:** A social listening tool that provides detailed insights into brand mentions, sentiment, and industry trends across social media platforms.
- **BuzzSumo:** A tool that identifies trending content and influencers in your industry, helping you create content that resonates with your audience.

Email Marketing and Automation Tools

- **Mailchimp:** A popular email marketing platform that integrates with social media for creating and managing email campaigns.
- **ActiveCampaign:** An email marketing and automation tool that offers advanced features for segmentation, personalization, and social media integration.
-

ConvertKit: An email marketing tool designed for creators, with features for building email lists and automating email sequences.

- **Zapier:** An automation tool that connects different apps and automates tasks, such as posting to social media when a new blog post is published.

Social Media Content Templates

Creating consistent, engaging content can be challenging, so here are some templates to help streamline the process. Customize these templates to fit your brand's voice, style, and objectives:

Content Calendar Template

A content calendar helps you plan and schedule your social media posts in advance, ensuring consistent and timely content delivery.

Date	Platform	Content Type	Post Topic/Title	Caption/Copy	Hashtags/Tags	Media/Links	Status
01/15/2024	Instagram	Image Post	Product Launch	"Excited to unveil our new..."	#ProductLaunch #NewArrivals	Image link	Scheduled
01/16/2024	Facebook	Video Post	Tutorial	"Learn how to use our latest..."	#Tutorial #HowTo	Video link	Draft

| 01/17/2024 | Twitter (X) | Text Post | Industry Insight | "Did you know that 80% of consumers..." | #Marketing #Trends | N/A | Posted |

Engagement Post Template

Use this template to craft posts that encourage audience engagement through questions, polls, or calls to action.

- **Post Title:** [Engage with Us]
- **Post Copy:** "We'd love to hear your thoughts! What's your favorite [product/feature] and why? Comment below and let us know."
- **Hashtags:** #Community #YourBrand #CustomerFavorites
- **Media:** [Include a relevant image, video, or graphic]
- **Call to Action:** "Share your opinion in the comments and tag a friend who would love [your product/service]!"

Promotional Post Template

This template is designed to promote products, services, or special offers on social media.

- **Post Title:** [Special Offer]
- **Post Copy:** "Get 20% off your next purchase with code SAVE20! Hurry, offer ends soon. Shop now and save big on our latest collection."

- **Hashtags:** #Sale #Discount #ShopNow #YourBrand
- **Media:** [Include product images, a promotional video, or a banner graphic]
- **Call to Action:** "Tap the link in our bio to shop the sale before it's gone!"

Storytelling Post Template

Use this template to share a story that connects with your audience on an emotional level.

- **Post Title:** [Behind the Scenes]
- **Post Copy:** "Every great product has a story. Here's how [Your Brand] started with just a dream and a passion for [industry]. We're proud to be where we are today, thanks to the support of amazing customers like you."
- **Hashtags:** #OurStory #BehindTheScenes #YourBrandJourney
- **Media:** [Include photos, videos, or a timeline graphic]
- **Call to Action:** "What's your story with [Your Brand]? Share it with us in the comments!"

Case Studies and Success Stories

Real-world examples of brands that have successfully implemented social media strategies can provide inspiration and valuable insights. Here are a few case studies that highlight different aspects of social media marketing success:

Case Study 1: Nike – The Power of User-Generated Content

Overview: Nike has long been a leader in social media marketing, particularly in leveraging user-generated content (UGC) to build community and brand loyalty.

Strategy: Nike encourages its customers to share their stories, achievements, and experiences with the brand using hashtags like #JustDoIt and #Nike. The brand regularly features UGC on its social media profiles, showcasing real customers and athletes using Nike products.

Results: This strategy has helped Nike create a strong sense of community and authenticity. By featuring real people, Nike's social media presence feels more relatable and genuine, leading to higher engagement and customer loyalty.

Key Takeaway: UGC can significantly boost engagement and trust in your brand. Encourage your customers to share their experiences and highlight their content to create a more authentic connection with your audience.

Case Study 2: Glossier – Building a Brand Through Social Listening

Overview: Glossier, a beauty brand, has built its entire business model on customer feedback and social listening, creating products that directly respond to what their audience wants.

Strategy: Glossier actively listens to its audience on social media, paying close attention to comments, reviews, and conversations. The brand uses this feedback to inform product development, marketing strategies, and even packaging decisions.

Results: By prioritizing customer input, Glossier has cultivated a highly engaged and loyal community. The brand's approach to social listening has also led to the creation of products that are in high demand, as they are tailored to the specific needs and desires of their customers.

Key Takeaway: Social listening is a powerful tool for understanding your audience and creating products and campaigns that resonate. Engage with your audience regularly and use their feedback to drive your business decisions.

Case Study 3: Airbnb – Mastering Video Content

Overview: Airbnb uses video content to tell compelling stories and create emotional connections with its audience. The brand's videos showcase the unique experiences that guests can have when staying in Airbnb properties.

Strategy: Airbnb produces high-quality video content that highlights the personal stories of hosts and guests. These videos are shared across social media platforms and are often part of larger campaigns that emphasize the sense of belonging and adventure that Airbnb offers.

Results: Airbnb's video content has significantly increased brand awareness and engagement. The emotional storytelling approach resonates with viewers, making the brand's content highly shareable and memorable.

Key Takeaway: Video content is an effective way to tell your brand's story and connect with your audience on a deeper level. Invest in high-quality videos that showcase the unique aspects of your brand and the experiences it offers.

Case Study 4: Starbucks – Integrating Social Media with Offline Campaigns

Overview: Starbucks has successfully integrated its social media marketing with offline campaigns to create a cohesive brand experience.

Strategy: Starbucks often launches campaigns that blend online and offline elements. For example, the #RedCupContest encourages customers to share photos of their holiday-themed Starbucks cups on social media. The brand also uses QR codes in-store to link to exclusive online content or promotions.

Results: These integrated campaigns have helped Starbucks drive both in-store traffic and online engagement. By creating a seamless experience across channels, Starbucks strengthens its brand presence and fosters customer loyalty.

Key Takeaway: Integrate your social media efforts with offline campaigns to create a more comprehensive and engaging brand experience. Use social media to amplify in-store promotions and encourage online engagement.

These appendices provide additional tools, resources, and examples to help you successfully implement the strategies discussed in this book. Whether you're just starting your social media journey or looking to refine your existing efforts, these resources will support your ongoing success in building and growing your brand online.

References

To deepen your understanding of social media marketing and related topics, here's a list of recommended books, articles, and research papers that have informed the content of this book. These resources provide valuable insights, strategies, and data to help you succeed in the ever-evolving digital landscape.

Books

1. **"Jab, Jab, Jab, Right Hook: How to Tell Your Story in a Noisy Social World" by Gary Vaynerchuk**
    - A comprehensive guide on how to create content that cuts through the noise on social media and delivers your brand's message effectively.
1. **"Contagious: How to Build Word of Mouth in the Digital Age" by Jonah Berger**
    - This book explores the science behind why certain content goes viral and how to create content that is more likely to be shared.
1. **"Crushing It!: How Great Entrepreneurs Build Their Business and Influence—and How You Can, Too" by Gary Vaynerchuk**
    - A follow-up to Vaynerchuk's earlier work, this book provides practical advice on building a personal brand through social media.
1. **"Building a StoryBrand: Clarify Your Message So Customers Will Listen" by Donald Miller**
    -

Miller's book focuses on the power of storytelling in marketing and how to craft a compelling brand narrative that resonates with your audience.

1. **"The Art of Social Media: Power Tips for Power Users" by Guy Kawasaki and Peg Fitzpatrick**
   - A practical guide with actionable tips for optimizing your social media strategy and maximizing your brand's online presence.

1. **"Hug Your Haters: How to Embrace Complaints and Keep Your Customers" by Jay Baer**
   - Baer's book provides insights into managing customer feedback and complaints on social media, turning negative experiences into opportunities for growth.

1. **"Made to Stick: Why Some Ideas Survive and Others Die" by Chip Heath and Dan Heath**
   - This book explores the principles that make ideas memorable and how to apply those principles to your marketing and social media content.

1. **"Epic Content Marketing: How to Tell a Different Story, Break through the Clutter, and Win More Customers by Marketing Less" by Joe Pulizzi**
   - Pulizzi's book emphasizes the importance of content marketing and how to create content that engages and converts.

1. **"Influence: The Psychology of Persuasion" by Robert B. Cialdini**
   - A classic in the field of marketing psychology, this book explains the principles of influence and how they can be applied to social media marketing.

1. **"Trust Me, I'm Lying: Confessions of a Media Manipulator" by Ryan Holiday**
   - Holiday's book offers a behind-the-scenes look at media manipulation and how brands can navigate the challenges of the modern media landscape.

Articles

1. **"The Impact of Social Media on Customer Behavior" by Kaplan and Haenlein (2010)**
   - An academic exploration of how social media influences consumer behavior and the implications for marketing strategies.
   - Available in *Business Horizons* journal.
2. **"The Power of Like: How Brands Reach (and Influence) Fans Through Social Media Marketing" by Sarah Hofstetter (2016)**
   - This article discusses the effectiveness of social media marketing in building brand loyalty and driving consumer engagement.
   - Published in *Journal of Interactive Marketing*.
3. **"Social Media and the Evolution of Transparency: The New Rules of Branding" by Lisa Arthur (2018)**
   - An article that explores how transparency on social media impacts brand trust and customer relationships.
   - Featured on *Forbes* website.

1. **"How to Leverage User-Generated Content on Social Media" by Anna Crowe (2019)**
   - A practical guide to incorporating user-generated content into your social media strategy.
   - Available on *Search Engine Journal*.
2. **"The Role of AI in Transforming Social Media Marketing" by Bernard Marr (2020)**
   - This article explores how AI and machine learning are changing the landscape of social media marketing.
   - Published on *Forbes* website.
3. **"The Future of Social Media Marketing: 10 Trends to Watch" by Andrew Hutchinson (2021)**
   - A forward-looking piece on emerging trends in social media marketing and what they mean for brands.
   - Available on *Social Media Today*.
4. **"Social Commerce: The Future of Online Shopping" by Lauren Freedman (2021)**
   - An article discussing the rise of social commerce and its impact on consumer buying behavior.
   - Published on *eMarketer*.
5. **"The Power of Video in Social Media Marketing" by Lisa Marcyes (2018)**
   - This article highlights the growing importance of video content in social media marketing and best practices for leveraging it.

- Available on *Hootsuite Blog*.
1. **"Why Social Media Influencers Are More Important Than Ever" by Pam Moore (2020)**
    - A deep dive into the role of influencers in modern marketing and how brands can effectively collaborate with them.
    - Published on *Marketing Nutz*.
1. **"Integrating Social Media with SEO: A Guide to Better Search Rankings" by Neil Patel (2019)**
    - Patel's article offers insights into how social media can enhance your SEO efforts and improve your search rankings.
    - Available on *Neil Patel Blog*.

Research Papers

1. **"Social Media Marketing: A Literature Review and Implications" by Felix, Rauschnabel, and Hinsch (2017)**
    - This paper reviews existing research on social media marketing and provides insights into effective strategies and future research directions.
    - Published in *Journal of Business Research*.
1. **"Consumer Engagement in Social Media: A Literature Review" by Brodie et al. (2013)**
    - A comprehensive review of consumer engagement in social media and its implications for marketing.

- Available in *Journal of Service Management*.

1. **"The Impact of Social Media on Brand Loyalty: The Case of Facebook" by Akrimi and Khemakhem (2014)**
   - This study examines how social media interactions on Facebook influence brand loyalty among consumers.
   - Published in *International Journal of Marketing Studies*.

1. **"Exploring the Role of Social Media in Digital Marketing" by Tuten and Solomon (2017)**
   - A research paper that explores the integration of social media into digital marketing strategies and its effects on consumer behavior.
   - Available in *Journal of Marketing Communications*.

1. **"The Effect of Social Media Advertising on Consumer Brand Loyalty" by Erdogmus and Cicek (2012)**
   - This paper investigates the impact of social media advertising on consumer loyalty to brands.
   - Published in *Procedia - Social and Behavioral Sciences*.

1. **"Social Media as a Marketing Tool: A Literature Review" by Edosomwan et al. (2011)**
   - A literature review on the use of social media as a marketing tool, discussing its benefits, challenges, and best practices.
   -

Published in *Journal of Business & Economic Research*.

1. **"Brand Communities on Social Media: A Study of Facebook and Twitter" by Muniz and O'Guinn (2014)**
    - This research explores the dynamics of brand communities on social media and how they influence brand perception and loyalty.
    - Available in *Journal of Consumer Research*.

1. **"User-Generated Content and Its Impact on Brand Equity: A Study of Social Media" by Smith et al. (2012)**
    - A research paper analyzing the impact of user-generated content on brand equity and consumer trust.
    - Published in *Journal of Marketing Research*.

1. **"The Role of Influencers in Shaping Consumer Attitudes and Behavior on Social Media" by Hughes et al. (2019)**
    - This paper examines how social media influencers affect consumer attitudes and purchase intentions.
    - Available in *Journal of Advertising*.

1. **"Social Media Strategies for Small Businesses: A Case Study of Facebook" by Pentina and Koh (2012)**
    - A case study that investigates how small businesses can effectively use Facebook for marketing purposes.

Published in *Journal of Research in Interactive Marketing*.

These references provide a solid foundation for anyone looking to delve deeper into social media marketing, offering both practical advice and academic insights. They can serve as valuable resources for further study, strategic planning, and the implementation of effective social media marketing tactics.

www.ingramcontent.com/pod-product-compliance
Lightning Source LLC
Chambersburg PA
CBHW071059240526
45471CB00016B/2162